teach yourself...
Rhythm Jazz Guitar
a player's guide

Al Stevens

Copyright © 2017 Al Stevens. No part of this publication may be reproduced in any form or by any means without the prior written permission of the author.

Tunes given as examples in this book are either the author's original compositions or well-known works in the public domain. Fragments that demonstrate musical theory and structure and that are cited as part of copyrighted tunes do not include melodies or lyrics. The chord changes are what you will be learning and playing. If you want to learn melodies and lyrics, which you are encouraged to do, there are many recordings and *fake* and *real* books available for your purchase. Check Appendix C.

Mockingbird Songs & Stories

Mockingbird Songs & Stories
5020 Saturday Place, Cocoa, FL 32926

Cover art by William Stauffer.

Please send comments and questions to al@alstevens.com

Dedication

To the fond memory of Billy Van Riper, friend, great guitarist, humorist. We miss you.

Acknowledgments

Many thanks to Sean Lohse and Lee Cornell whose comments and criticisms added substantially to the content of this book.

And to Chuck Van Riper for the picture of Billy.

Special thanks to Judy whose patience lets me work and whose diligence keeps me going.

Description

teach yourself... Rhythm Jazz Guitar guides you as you learn the basics of playing jazz chords.

This book is for student and experienced guitarists who want to move into the realm of jazz accompaniment. You learn a basic repertoire of chord sequences that employ colorful, or hip, voicings. The sequences use chord fingerings that are easy to play, with each chord in comfortable proximity on the fretboard to the previous and next ones.

You learn to translate those cryptic chord symbols you see on sheet music and big band charts into easily-fingered chords that involve no extreme hand stretches, sound good, and fit into the harmonic context of the tune you're playing. With the knowledge you learn in this book and a disciplined regimen of practice, you will be equipped with skills and tools that not only allow you to sit in at informal jam sessions but to expand your knowledge into the more advanced realms of jazz guitar playing.

Books by Al Stevens

Stanley Bentworth Mysteries Omnibus Books 1 - 3
Diabetics Behaving Badly
On the Street Where You Die (Stanley Bentworth mysteries: Book 1)
A Dead Ringer (Stanley Bentworth mysteries: Book 2)
Clueless (Stanley Bentworth mysteries: Book 3)
The Rat Squad (Stanley Bentworth mysteries: Book 4)
White Collar Murders (Stanley Bentworth mysteries: Book 5)
Fugitive Warrant (Stanley Bentworth mysteries: Book 6)
Hooker Stalker Killer Pimp (Stanley Bentworth mysteries: Book 7)
Murder in the Bermuda Triangle (Stanley Bentworth mysteries: Book 8)
Assisted Homicide (Stanley Bentworth mysteries: Book 9)
Corpsicles' Cremains (Stanley Bentworth mysteries: Book 10)
Annie Somewhere
The Shadow on the Grassy Knoll
Confessions of a Cat Burglar (free book, referenced in A Dead Ringer)
Off the Wall Stories
Golden Eagle's Final Flight (with Ron Skipper)
Ventriloquism: Art, Craft, Profession
Politically Incorrect Scripts for Comedy Ventriloquists
Welcome to Programming
Teach Yourself C++ 7th Edition

...and more computer programming and usage books.

Table of Contents

PART I. Getting Started...1
Chapter 1. Introduction..2
   Who are You?...2
   What do You Need?..2
   What's in this Book?...2
   Visual Depictions of Music...3
   The Changes..4
   Accompaniment..4
   Who am I?..4
Chapter 2. Jazz Guitar...6
   Jazz Guitarists...6
   Traditional Guitar Music..6
   Jazz Guitar Music...6
   Why the Guitar?...7
   Why Jazz?...7
   Jazz and Standards...7
Chapter 3. Your Guitar..8
   Fret Numbering..8
   String Numbering...9
   Tuning..10
   The Capo...11
PART II. Chords..12
Chapter 4. Chord Basics..13
   Chords...13
   Chord Symbols...13
   The Root Note..15
   Finding the Root Notes..16
   Forms..17
   Basic Chords..17
   Inversions..20
   Slash Chords..21
   Barre..21
   Strumming..22
   Plucking..23
   Rhythm Playing...23
Chapter 5. Notation..24
   Accidentals..24
   Standard Notation..24
   Grid Notation...25
   Tablature...26
   Lead Sheet Notation..26

- Slash Notation..27
- Rhythmic Notation...27
- Nashville Number System..28
- Internet Notation..29
- Summary..29

Chapter 6. Transposable Forms..30
- Transposables with Open Strings...30
- A Tradition...31

Chapter 7. Other Essential Chords..32
- Diminished...32
- Half Diminished (min7♭5)...35
- Augmented...36
- Augmented 7..37
- Suspended..37
- Flatted Fifth (♭5)..38
- Sharp Eleven (♯11)...38
- Sharp Nine (♯9)...39
- Flat Nine (♭9)..39
- Alternate (Alt)...40
- Walking Bass Lines...40

PART III. Theory...43

Chapter 8. Theory 101..44
- Octaves...44
- Intervals...44
- Half Tones..44
- Scales...45
- Chord Resolutions..47
- Chord Changes...50

Chapter 9. Chord Colors...53
- Vanilla Chords..53
- Colorful Chords..54
- 9 and 13..54
- 6, Maj7, and 6/9..55
- Vanilla vs Colors..56

Chapter 10. Tonal Centers..57

PART IV. Changes...59

Chapter 11. Two-Five-One...60
- ii-V-I Major..60
- Cherokee Bridge...66
- Summary Chord Grids...66
- ii-V-i in Minor Keys..68

Chapter 12. One-Six-Two-Five..70

Chapter 13. The Blues..72
- Major Blues..72

- Minor Blues 74
- Non-blues Blues 74

Chapter 14. Rhythm Changes 75
Chapter 15. Passages 78
- The Chorus 78
- Intros 79
- Verses 80
- Turnarounds 80
- Bridge 80
- Endings 83

Chapter 16. Substitutions 88
- The Blues Redux 88
- Preceding Minor 7 90
- Tritone Substitution 90
- Flatted Fifth Descent 92
- Alternative Reharmonizations 92

PART V. Charts 94
Chapter 17. Chord Charts 95
- Title 96
- Staves 96
- Clef Sign 96
- Key Signature 96
- Time Signature 97
- Measures 97
- Tempo 97

Chapter 18. Rhythmic Notation 98
Chapter 19. Big Band Charts 101
- A Chart to Study 101
- Rehearsal Numbers 102
- Navigation 103
- Interpretation 105
- A Walk Through the Chart 109

PART VI. Playing 111
Chapter 20. Freddie 112
Chapter 21. Comping 116
Chapter 22. Improvisation 118
- Listen to the Improvisers 119
- Try to Improvise 119
- Hum Your Improvisation 119
- Match Notes and Chords 120
- Playing Outside 120
- Blue Notes 120
- Arpeggios and Scales 121
- Licks 122

- Quotes 122
- Impromptu Composition 123
- Transcriptions 123
- Reward and Punishment 124
- Chapter 23. Practicing 125
- Appendix A: Chords 131
  - Using this Appendix 131
  - The Chords 132
  - Summary 139
- Appendix B: Jazz Slang 140
- Appendix C. Resources 142
  - Links 142
  - Books 142
- From the Author 143

PART I. Getting Started

Welcome to *teach yourself... Rhythm Jazz Guitar,* a guide with which you teach yourself the basics of playing jazz chords on guitar for vocal and instrumental accompaniments.

This is Part I, and it gets you started with a touch of jazz guitar background and what I think you need in order to proceed with these lessons. It's the usual who are you, who am I, what this book is about filler that every how-to book includes. But it also introduces the musical presentation conventions these lessons employ to portray guitar chords and chord charts, so maybe you shouldn't skip it.

Chapter 1. Introduction

We'll begin by addressing what you should expect to learn from this book, what methods and gear we use to teach and learn, and who I am and why I'm qualified to teach you to be a rhythm jazz guitarist.

Who are You?

You're a guitar player with some level of proficiency in non-jazz idioms, and you want to expand your playing to accompany jazz tunes and standards, perhaps in a big band. But in terms of playing jazz chords, rhythms, and accompaniments, you're a relative newcomer to this style of guitar playing.

What do You Need?

Obviously you need a guitar (Chapter 3). But you also need to bring a few other things to the project.

Software

I strongly suggest that you purchase the program named *Band-In-A-Box* from http://www.pgmusic.com and download the free practice backing tracks from my website at http://www.alstevens.com/jazzguitar. More about all that in Chapter 23.

And, of course, you'll need a computer on which to run the program and with which to play the backing tracks.

Goals

As an aspiring jazz guitarist, you typically wish to play jazz or old standards and accompany singers (yourself, perhaps) and/or other instrument players. If you have lofty goals—to play like Joe Pass or Pat Martino, for example—good for you. This book does not come close to teaching the way, but it can be your first step.

Dedication, Drive and Motivation

Finally, to become a proficient jazz guitarist, you must have the time and desire to learn. You must be motivated and willing to practice.

Of course, anything worth doing well requires effort. There are challenges. With practice you can get past them, and if you work at it, eventually you'll be playing along with the pros.

That notwithstanding, don't give up your life to this dream unless playing guitar is all that matters to you. Don't forsake your family, your health, or your community. Don't obsess.

What's in this Book?

Check out this list. These are what you can expect to learn from the lessons and exercises here.

- You will learn a basic repertoire of chord changes as they are used in jazz in the keys that jazz players play in.

- The chords employ easy fingerings, with no hand stretches beyond the reach of an adult guitarist with relatively small hands.

- You will learn to translate cryptic chord symbols on sheet music and big band charts into easily-fingered chord forms.

- You will learn basic music theory, enough to play rhythm guitar in a jazz environment. Unlike many works on guitar chords this one does not simply provide chord symbols and grids so you can look them up when you encounter them on charts. I try to explain *why* the chords sound right and, sometimes, hip in the harmonic contexts in which you play them.

- The book includes chapters on comping, improvisation, and how to read chord charts and navigate big band charts. The coverage is not wall-to-wall. Those subjects could be books unto themselves and they are. Here you get an introduction to and a taste for what you can be doing after you've finished the lessons in this book.

Because of my background, examples in this book draw upon old standard tunes, many of which are a part of the jazz literature. Jazz musicians have adopted the compositions of Gershwin, Porter, Rogers, and the many tin pan alley composers, into the jazz literature. You can listen to renditions of them on YouTube, and you can download backing tracks and chord chart PDFs to support your practice of such tunes from http://www.alstevens.com/jazzguitar.

Visual Depictions of Music

Writing a book of prose and pictures that teaches something audible is difficult to say the least. Learning from such a book can be a challenge. Ideally, you would augment these printed lessons with one-on-one instruction from a human teacher. I don't know if that's possible for you or even whether you want to do it. So I've tried to make this book stand alone as a way for you to teach yourself rhythm jazz guitar. Consequently, you will learn from two visual sources.

Grids and Tabs

You will learn about chords and how to play them from pictorial grids and tabs that depict how to finger each chord on the fretboard. Here's an example of one such chord so depicted:

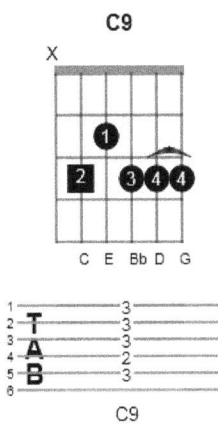

If you've ever looked at commercial sheet music, you've seen grids above the staves along with the chord symbols. Music publishers used to include them so that amateur guitar players could strum along around the fireside or kitchen table. This was in the days when home entertainment didn't get much more technical than a player piano and a radio.

Chord Charts

You will learn how to play music—tunes—from chord charts that depict when to play each chord based on its symbol and its position on the chart. Here's an example of a tune as shown on a chord chart:

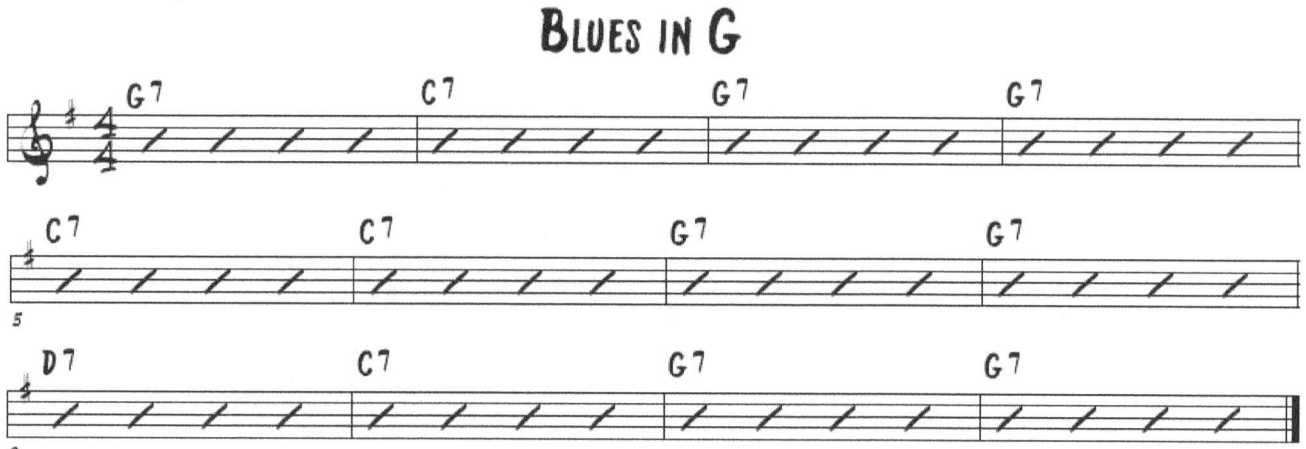

Those cryptic letters and numbers—G7, C7, etc.—above the staves are *chord symbols,* the names of the chords. By the time you see your next chord chart in these lessons, you will have learned several ways to play each chord on the chart and you will play tunes by selecting from those ways based on the chord symbols. If that looks hard, don't worry. It all comes clear as you progress through the lessons. If you should happen to see a chord symbol that hasn't been explained, refer to Appendix A to see how to play it.

The Changes

We discuss *chord progressions* and *chord sequences*. They are the same thing, meaning a set of chords played one after the other to achieve a harmonic objective. Jazz musicians typically call these sets *chord changes* or, simply, *changes*. We'll tend to use this idiom because that's what you'll hear on the bandstand.

Accompaniment

Accompaniment is playing background music to accompany a singer, solo instrument, or even a complete band. *Rhythm accompaniment* is playing patterns of chords that keep time, typically four beats to the measure at the tempo chosen for the tune. *Comping* (Chapter 21) is, for this discussion, playing accompanying chords not necessarily in strict four-beat time, but with player-chosen rhythmic patterns and beats.

Note that other works on this subject address comping as including four-beat playing, but I differentiate them for the sake of convenience.

There are other rhythmic jazz time and tempo styles that you must eventually learn, such as waltzes and Latin rhythms, but they should come natural to you after you've completed these lessons and gotten some playing experience. For now, we'll stick to swinging four-beat and ballads.

Who am I?

I'm a retired professional musician and writer with about 60 years playing gigs ranging from piano bars to concert halls, night clubs to weddings, private parties to international jazz festivals, cruise ships, and even the occasional outdoor strawberry and frog legs festival.

teach yourself Rhythm Jazz Guitar, *a player's guide* – Al Stevens

I play several instruments at performance levels. Not a virtuoso mind you, but a competent sideman. Here's a picture of yours truly playing my first guitar.

That Harmony was a hand-me-down and I still have it. I have several others, all more playable than the old Harmony, which hangs on my studio wall next to a lamp I made from my first trumpet, which are always there lest I forget my humble roots.

This is me now with a newer guitar. It's the Epiphone that lured me back into playing guitar after a many-year layoff.

Nowadays, I'm off the road for good. I stick to the studio, playing for my own entertainment, taking the occasional evening to visit the old haunts, sit in with jam sessions, and generally enjoy myself. I also do a lot of writing: music, mysteries, and how-to books like this one.

Chapter 2. Jazz Guitar

Jazz played on guitar is as old as jazz itself. Pictures of early jazz bands typically include a guitar player in the rhythm section. Here's a band led by legendary trumpet player Buddy Bolden.

The *Bolden Band* used a guitar for rhythm and chords. This might be the first picture ever taken of what today would be called a *jazz band*. Buddy is standing in the back row behind the guitar player.

Jazz Guitarists

There are many great rhythm jazz guitar pioneers now gone from us. You can find their recordings online. Among them are George Van Eps, Charlie Christian, Eddie Condon, Django Reinhardt, Al Casey, Steve Jordon, and many others. Chapter 20 is dedicated to the playing style of Freddie Green, the standard-bearer for big band rhythm guitar.

Those guys are gone but they have many extant successors, great rhythm jazz guitarists who inspire and influence our playing, among them, Marty Grosz, Howard Alden, Bucky Pizzarelli, and so on.

Traditional Guitar Music

The guitar is friendly to those who play simple chord structures and use a capo (Chapter 3). Early rock 'n' roll, folk music, gospel, and country-western tunes used simple three-chord structures, and were relatively easy compared to more complicated music genres. If you could play the G chord, the C chord, and the D7 chord, knew the 12-bar blues chord changes (Chapter 13), and owned a capo, you could keep up with most C&W and rock bands in the old days.

Jazz Guitar Music

Jazz is more complex than traditional rock 'n' roll and C&W. It often deviates from their simple harmonic constructs. No matter what key signature you begin with, in jazz you can find yourself coming up against the chord changes of any of the other key signatures. Standard tunes such as *You Go to My Head*, *The Man I Love*, and *Have You Met Miss Jones*, and jazz classics such as *Joy Spring*, *I Remember Clifford*, and *'Round Midnight* are all over the tonal center map (Chapter 10). Which means you need to be able to play in every key, which further means you need to know how to play the chords in all the tonal centers within the twelve-tone scale. Don't be intimidated. It's not as difficult as it sounds. But you must practice.

Why the Guitar?

The guitar is, in my opinion, the perfect musical instrument. Like the piano, the guitar is a standalone instrument for solos and accompaniments. You don't need a rhythm section. The instrument supports everything: melody, chords, and rhythm.

And the guitar is truly portable. It begs to be played around a campfire, on a porch, in a canoe, even in an outhouse.

Why Jazz?

Why indeed? Why do musicians want to play jazz? Except for a few well-known performers, there's not much money being made playing jazz. There aren't many paying gigs, maybe because so many amateur musicians are so eager to play jazz that they take gigs for low pay or sit in for nothing. Club owners have become accustomed to paying from zero to squat for talent, and disk jockeys and karaoke operators have bumped live music into something from the past.

We jazz musicians are our own worst enemies and our own biggest fans. So why the enthusiasm among musicians to play jazz?

To the dedicated, motivated player, jazz is a calling, a passion, a need to stretch one's creativity beyond the printed page of notation to play what we hear, by ear, either alone or in collaboration with other jazz musicians.

And jazz music itself is compelling in ways that are difficult if not impossible to describe. When you hear it, you'll know. When you play it, you'll be hooked.

Jazz and Standards

We discuss the playing of *jazz* and *standard* tunes. That would seem to be a clear distinction, but there is a lot of overlap. Jazz tunes consist of pieces written usually by jazz musicians specifically for jazz performances. Often they don't have lyrics. Examples are *Joy Spring*, *Oleo*, *Blue Bossa*, and *Take Five*. Standard tunes, on the other hand, are tunes from the so-called "Great American Songbook" and they include show tunes, tin pan alley, and some contemporary pop tunes. Many of them have been assimilated into the jazz repertoire and have become de facto jazz standards. Examples are *Stardust*, *There Will Never Be Another You*, *Just the Way You Are*, and virtually any tune written by Duke Ellington.

Chapter 3. Your Guitar

Obviously, the lessons in this book expect you to have a guitar. It doesn't matter what kind of guitar. It can be an acoustic steel or nylon string guitar, an electric, or an acoustic electric of any make, size or body style. You can have a beat-up old box or a shiny new latest model. It can be expensive or you might have picked it up at a yard sale. The lessons here assume your guitar has six strings and the conventional guitar tuning of E, A, D, G, B, E. We don't get into whammy bars, distortion, or effects pedals, so it doesn't matter whether your setup supports those features. You aren't required to have a pick, a capo, a strap, an amplifier, or long hair and tattoos. All you need is a guitar.

Eventually, when you start playing with groups from small to big bands, you'll need a guitar amplifier. For now, unless your guitar is a solid body electric, you can get by going acoustic.

Every guitar book must include an illustration that shows you the parts of your guitar and their names, so here it is:

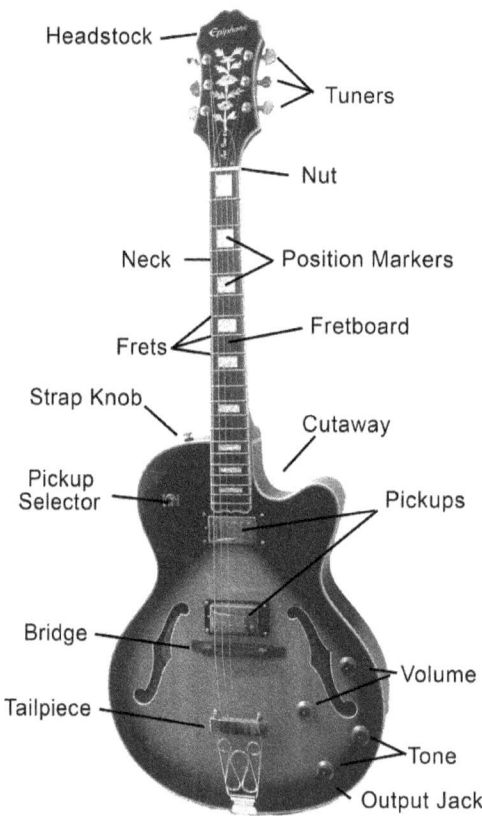

This picture, however, is of *my* guitar. Yours is probably different, but they all have things in common. If I mention a guitar part by name and you don't know what it is, check here.

Fret Numbering

The guitar has a characteristic that, when discussed, can lead to misunderstandings. That characteristic is how the fretboard is oriented. Consider this illustration which shows a portion of the fretboard and the fret numbers.

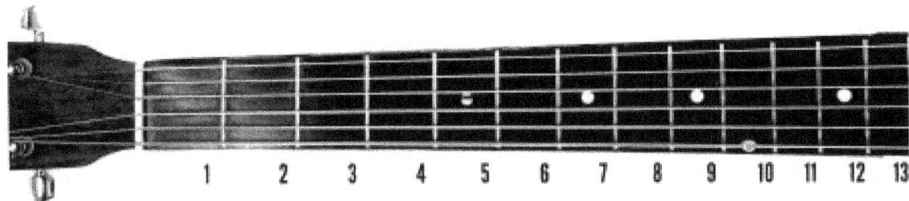

The frets are numbered left to right in ascending order, which works because that's how we read printed text, and the pitches of notes are higher as we move to the next higher fret on the same string. Now consider this grid, the means by which we represent chords pictorially.

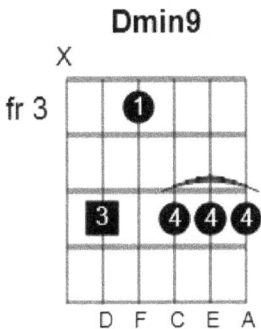

The grid depicts a section of the fretboard as it would be if you turned the guitar upright with the headstock at the top. In this position the fret numbers ascend as we look at frets lower in the picture.

The confusion comes in when we speak of the "next higher" or "next lower" fret. In all cases, these references in this book refer to the direction of the fret number and the pitch rather than the grid's orientation on the page.

Frets are the metal strips embedded into the *fretboard,* also called the *fingerboard.* This book shows diagrams such as the one above of chords with fingers pressing strings to the fingerboard itself between the frets, which makes contact between the string and the next higher fret. This is conventional notation for these grid diagrams. Most players press their fingers as close to or directly onto the frets themselves.

String Numbering

There's a similar anomaly in how strings are numbered. The numbers go from 1 to 6 starting at the highest pitched string. So when we say "lower string," it's not always clear whether we're referring to a lower-pitched string or one with a lower number. I try to avoid ambiguity in these lessons by calling each string by its number—string 1, string 2, and so on—and hoping you know what I mean. If you are unsure, refer to a tab (Chapter 5) as shown here:

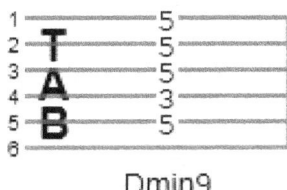

The strings in the tab are laid out the way they would appear with the guitar in your lap facing up.

Tuning

An old musician's joke goes like this:

> *During a rehearsal for a jazz combo, the guitarist took time between every number to tune his guitar. The other players were annoyed at what they thought to be a waste of time. One of them said, "I attended a solo concert of Andrés Segovia in the old days and he played the entire program without retuning once. The guitar player sloughed it off and said, "Well, some cats just don't give a damn."*

Most of you won't need this discussion; you already know how to tune your guitar. But for those whose status as a newcomer is more elementary, here are the basics of getting your axe tuned up.

First, in an ensemble, you have to be in tune with the others. Using a meter is okay but be careful about that. Make sure the meter is properly calibrated to A=440. If you use a meter app in your smart phone, you must isolate yourself from the racket that fills the stand while everyone sets up. A smart phone has no phone jack for your cable, so it hears everything in the room. It's best to use a meter that has an input jack.

A=440 means that the note A is tuned to 440 cycles per second. Most meters allow you to select ranges in that neighborhood in case, for instance, the piano is out. Your best bet is to tune to that pitch by ear and then tune the other strings using the procedure given below.

Make sure the other players use the same point of reference for tuning their instruments. If you are in perfect tune and the others aren't, the music suffers.

If there's an acoustic piano (as opposed to an electronic keyboard), check its tuning. Acoustic pianos are often our of tune. They might sound great but if they're not tuned to A=440, your meter is no help unless you can calibrate the meter to the piano's pitch.

> *In the days before portable pianos, the band was checking out the setup at a new venue when the piano player realized the piano was a half-tone off. He called the owner over and told him, "This piano can't be used."*
>
> *The owner replied, "What's wrong with it? I just had it painted."*

Make sure no one has adjusted the electronic keyboard's pitch with its transposition function setting. When in doubt, reset the keyboard by powering it off then back on.

The guitar is tuned to the notes E, A, D, G, B, E, starting at string 6 and tuning strings 5, 4, 3, 2, and 1 in succession, following these steps:

1. Get the first note, the low E on string 6, in tune with your band's common reference, which might be the piano or the lead guitar.

2. Tune string 5, open, A, to string 6, fret 5.

3. Tune string 4, open, D, to string 5, fret 5.

4. Tune string 3, open, G, to string 4 fret 5.

5. Tune string 2, open, B, to string 3, fret 4. Observe that this tuning moves your left hand down a fret.

6. Move your hand back up to fret 5 and tune string 1, open, E, to string 2, fret 5.

7. Check the E, string 1, open, against the piano or lead guitar.

8. Iterate steps 1 through 6 until it's perfect.

Eventually, with experience, you'll be able to tune the strings all open by ear from the band's common reference note.

Concert bands and jazz combos tune from a common B♭. Concert orchestras tune from A.

The Capo

A *capo* is a device you attach to the guitar's neck at a chosen fret so you can play the chord forms you know on the higher frets. The capo in effect moves the nut up the fretboard, and your G chord becomes, successively, an A♭ chord, an A chord, a B♭ chord and so on.

A guitarist might use a capo to transpose his or her playing to accompany singers who, because of their vocal ranges, prefer keys other than the originals—which describes most female singers.

> *Glenn Campbell is quoted as having said the capo allowed him to pursue a successful career as a studio guitarist long before he became a celebrity vocalist.*

Jazz musicians tend to look down upon capos as being "training wheels" much like the transposition function on electronic keyboards.

> *Q: Why did the arranger put a rubato passage and a fermata at the beginning and end of the bridge to* Body and Soul?"
>
> *A: To give the guitar player time to re-position the capo.*

You will not need a capo to learn the lessons in this book. In fact, I'd rather you never used one. I'd rather you learned to make any chord by using its several forms and positions on the fretboard.

There are valid applications for the use of a capo. Rhythm jazz guitar is not one of them.

PART II. Chords

The foundation of rhythm jazz guitar is found in the chords you play as accompaniment to the rest of the musical entourage whether that be you as a solo vocalist, in a duo, a combo, or a big band. Part II begins your learning of how chords work on the guitar and in jazz. There's a lot to know, and you'll learn more in later parts. Part II gets you started by explaining the basics of how chords work and how they are depicted visually so guitar players know which ones to play at any given place in a musical presentation.

Chapter 4. Chord Basics

This discussion explains chords and how to play them. You probably already know some of this, but look it over to make sure we're speaking the same language.

Chords

A *chord* is two or more different notes played at the same time. When you strum or pluck guitar strings, you're playing a chord. Which chord you play depends on which frets you press on which strings and which other strings are open (played but not pressed). The chord consists of the various notes that are played in that combination.

Here is the ever-popular C chord, the triad of notes C, E, and G.

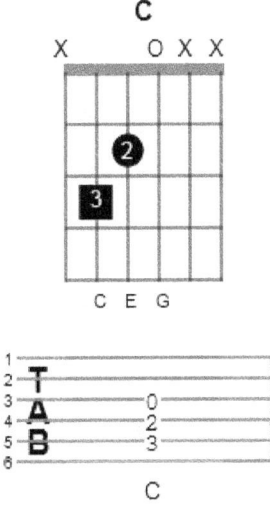

A *triad* is a chord with three notes in it consisting of the root note, the 3rd and the 5th. It is the basis for virtually all the chords you will learn in these lessons.

Chordal instruments—those that play more than one note at a time, such as virtually any stringed or keyboard instrument—can play chords alone. Wind and vocal ensembles combine the notes of multiple instruments each played by individual musicians to form chords.

> *I was teaching basic music theory to an elementary school music class, and I asked the question, "Why do you suppose we have chords?"*
>
> *A little girl held her hand up and answered, "So everyone doesn't have to play the same note."*

I can't improve on that explanation.

Chord Symbols

Most guitar notation includes *chord symbols* somewhere on the chart. Eventually, the chord symbols should be all you need to strum along from a chart.

Chord symbols are what you see above the staff on lead sheets, sheet music, and big band charts. More about that later.

There are many variations of how chords are named, and there are many chord symbols that you won't need to know to get through this book. For an exhaustive treatment of the subject, search Wikipedia for "chord names." I promise you'll come hurrying back here after you read way more than you ever wanted or needed to know.

Here are the elements of chord symbols as we use them:

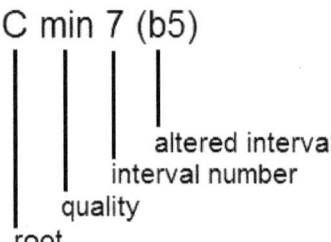

The example in the illustration contains most of the components of the chord symbols that we use.

Root

A chord symbol always begins with the name of the note that is its *root*. In the illustration, C is the root of the chord. Everything past that expands on the root. If there is only the root, the chord is assumed to be a major triad with the root note at its beginning. You'll learn more about the root later in this chapter.

Quality

The *quality* defines the chord as being major, minor, diminished, augmented, suspended, or major seventh using these tokens:

- maj (implied so typically omitted)
- min
- dim
- aug
- sus
- maj7

You'll learn about these chord qualities as the lessons progress.

Some chord naming conventions abbreviate minor chords with a lower-case 'm' instead of 'min.' That's a common practice. Some use a simple dash (-) to indicate a minor chord. Here are several various ways you might see, for example, a G minor chord symbol:

- Gm
- Gmin
- G-

Interval Number

The interval number identifies a note that is not part of the chord's triad but that is included in the chord's voicing. Rather than use the added note's name, chord symbols use interval numbers relative to the scale of the root note. This number can be 6, 7, 9, 11, or 13. You'll learn what these numbers mean as you use chords that employ them in the exercises that follow.

Altered Interval

An altered interval, usually but not always shown in parentheses, specifies that one of the chord's notes is to be sharped or flatted. The note is also a number interval relative to the root's major scale. For example, the (♭5) altered interval in the illustration specifies that the fifth of the chord, G in this example, is to be flatted.

Standards?

I've explained here how these lessons use chord symbol conventions that most jazz musicians will know immediately. There's more to it, however, and as you need to know more, we'll go into that.

There seem to be various ways to assign names to chord symbols. We have no established, recognized, and accepted standards for that.

For example, like the several ways to spell the quality value of a minor chord, there are other abbreviations or short-cuts. A delta character indicates a major7 chord, a lower-case superscript 'o' is a diminished chord, an 'o' with a horizontal slash through it is a minor 7 (♭5) chord, also called a a *half-diminished* chord, a plus (+) indicates an *augmented* chord.

The parentheses around the altered interval is intended to disambiguate what would otherwise be confusing notation. For example, A♭9 is an A♭ chord with a 9th added. But A(♭9) is an A chord with a flatted ninth. If there are no ambiguities, some copyists omit the parentheses. For example, B♭♯11 is unambiguous without the parentheses.

The apparent inconsistencies are a product of the evolutionary nature of musical notation. The differences came from multiple sources and times and were diversely accepted conventions by various musical cultures. They were evolving all over the place and musicians weren't always talking to one another about it. No one standard has ever taken hold or become *de facto*, and musicians have come to learn the various chord-naming idioms and to work with them.

This will, I hope, become apparent in Chapter 5.

If you are on the bandstand and you see an unfamiliar chord symbol, ask the other musicians. If they don't know, agree on a chord that fits the tune based on the notes they are all playing. If it's a so-called *head chart*, just agree on something that sounds right.

It isn't always precise or scientific, but after a while, you get used to it.

The Root Note

As you learned above, every chord has a *root* note, and that note is the first part of the chord symbol. The root note for Cmaj7, for example, is C. The root note for F7 is F. And so on.

You need to know the root so you can fit the chord into the harmonic context of the musical passages that you play. That's why the chord symbol, which is the chord's name, includes the chord's root note as its first part.

The grids we use in these lessons to represent chords use a black box instead of a black circle to represent the root.

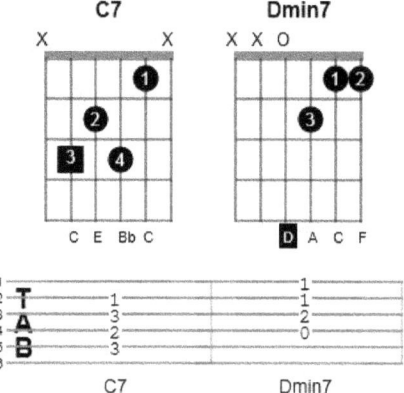

The C7 chord on the left shows that the note C is the root note of the chord. Observe that the chord has another C at string 2, fret 1. That note is the root too, but we depict only one root on a grid, usually the lowest pitched of the root notes.

If the root is an open string, as shown in the Dmin7 chord on the right above, the grids put the black box at the bottom of the grid on the root note's name.

Tablature (shown under the grids and discussed in Chapter 5) does not specifically identify the root note except by the chord symbol at the bottom of the tab, and that is not always given.

If the grid's chord does not include the root, it is a *rootless* chord, something we rarely use in these lessons, and there is, of course, no black box in the grid.

Chapter 20 includes examples of rootless chords.

Finding the Root Notes

These lessons teach you to play chords with root notes on the lowest-pitched string of the chord. Those root notes are played only on strings 6, 5, and 4.

There's a lot more to know about chords on a guitar, but this is where you'll start.

The grids used in this book to portray chords tell you which strings and frets are played for each root note. But eventually you'll be playing from chord symbols only, which do not tell you which notes to play except by name, and you'll need to know where those notes are on your fretboard.

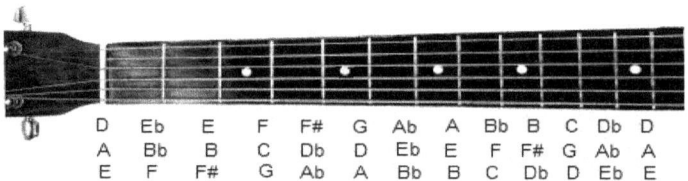

To help you find your notes, use this diagram. The rows of note names under the fretboard correspond to strings 4, 5, and six. The note names under the nut are the notes those strings sound when they are open—not pressed down. There are plenty more notes on a fretboard. This picture only goes up to fret 12 and only up to string 4. But these are where you'll find your roots.

Forms

The two chords shown here are different chords, but they share the same *form*, which means the same fingering. The difference is in which frets the form, and thus your hand, is positioned.

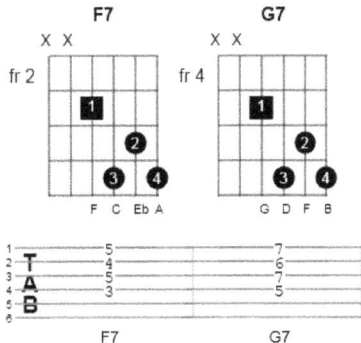

The fingering and placement of muted strings (depicted by Xs at the top of the grids) are the same for the two chords. Their form is just what you see in this example. It is the same for both chords. The difference between the grids, obscure as it may be, is found in the fret number in the grid's upper left corner.

Basic Chords

We start with four basic chords, the major, the minor, the dominant 7, and the minor 7. Most of your jazz playing will use these chords. We'll use three forms to make each chord, one each with the root on strings 6, 5 and 4. Since there are twelve possible root notes, that would be 144 chords. But we don't have to look at that many. You'll see why soon.

Major

A *major* chord is three notes, called a *triad*, that include the root note, the 3rd, and the 5th. Here is the C major scale, which you need to know to understand the C major chord.

C, D, E, F, G, A, B, C

A C major chord includes C, the root or first note in the scale, E, the 3rd note in the scale, and G, the 5th note in the scale. Here's the familiar C chord shown in a grid and tablature.

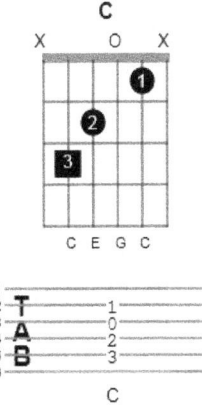

Each of these notes can occur more than once in the grid depending on the form of the chord.

Observe that C occurs twice in the chord pattern. It neither adds to nor detracts from the sound. You could mute string 2 and the harmonic sound would be the same.

These are three forms for the major chords, each one using a different string for the root note.

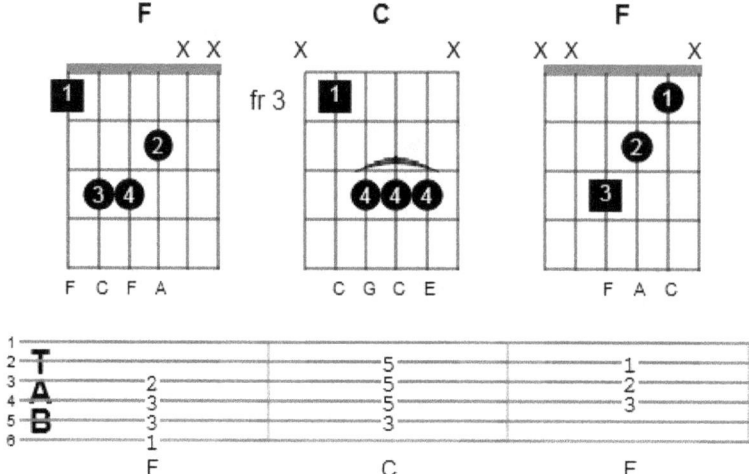

We've used roots F, C and F to keep your left hand close to the first fret position for now. The first F chord has an extra F note just for the convenience of finger placement. Without it, you'd have to mute string 4. The C chord has an extra C for the same reason.

Here's why we don't have to show you all the chords with all the roots. You can use these three forms and move your hand up the fretboard to make major chords with different roots. Chapter 6 discusses this practice in more detail.

Minor

A *minor* chord is the same as the major except the 3rd note is flatted (one half tone lower, one fret lower). In this case finger 2 is pulled down to fret 1.

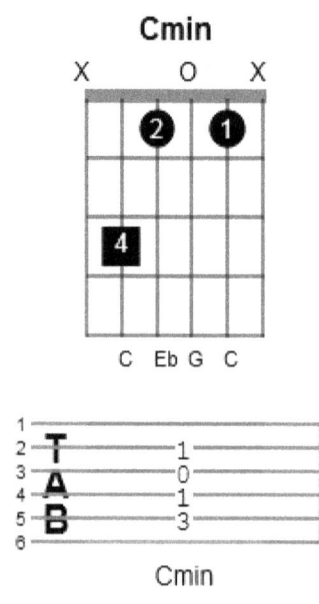

These are the three forms for minor chords, once again using F, C and F for the roots on strings 6, 5 and 4.

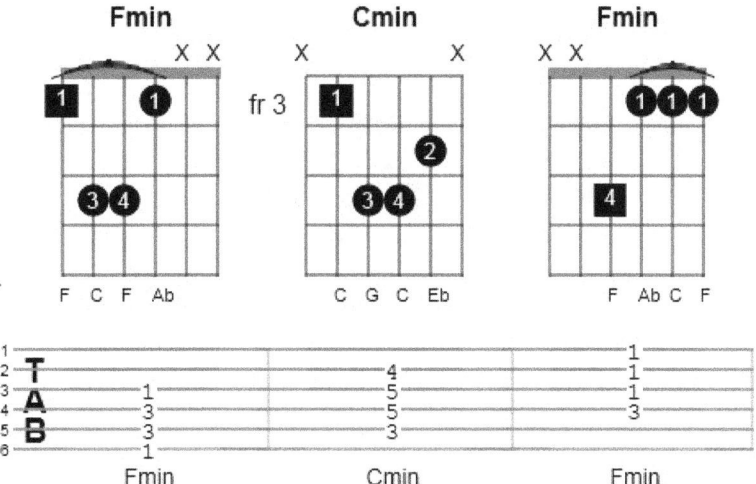

As with the major chords, you can move these forms up and down the fretboard to make more minor chords.

Dominant 7

The dominant 7 chord is a major triad that adds and flats the seventh note in the root's scale. Back to the C major scale.

C, D, E, F, G, A, B, C

The 7th note is B. When you lower the 7th note to the next half-tone down, in this case, B♭, you are turning the major chord into a *dominant* 7th. This chord would then be:

C, E, G, B♭

These are the three forms for dominant 7 chords with roots on strings 6, 5 and 4.

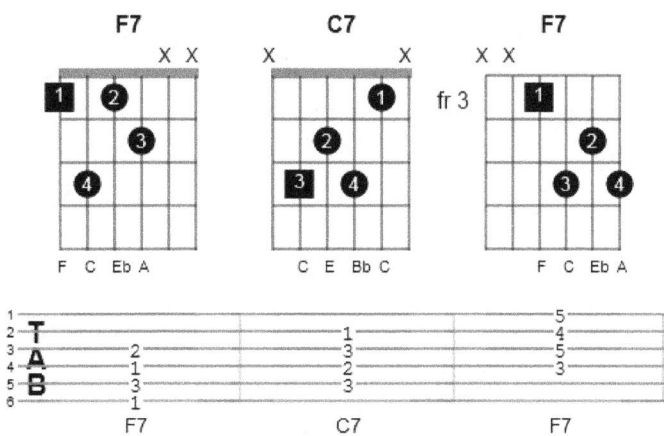

Once again, these fingerings work in any fret position to make other dominant 7 chords.

Observe that the C7 chord has no G in it, the 5th note of the C scale. That's okay. The 5th is the least necessary note in a dominant 7 chord. Nobody misses it when it isn't there. Later you'll learn to make a C9 chord, which includes all the notes and sounds better than a C7 anyway.

Minor 7

A minor 7 chord is a minor triad with the addition of the 7th note of the scale flatted. These are the three forms for the minor 7 chords.

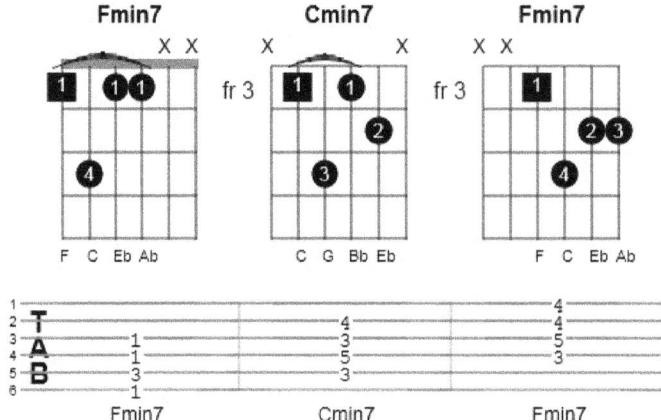

As with the other basic chords, these fingerings work in any fret position to make other minor 7 chords.

Inversions

The chords shown above place the root notes on the lowest-pitched string in the forms. That is the usual way chords are thought of by guitarists, pianists, and other chordal instrument players. But for each triad (for example) there are three ways to play it. The first way is called the *root position* and has the root note on the bottom as we've shown them so far. The other two ways are called *inversions*, which means that the lowest note played in the chord is other than the root.

The C chord's root position consists of the notes C, E, and G, beginning on the bottom. The *first* inversion is played E, G, and C, and the *second* inversion is played G, C, and E. Here is the C chord played in its root position and in both its inversions.

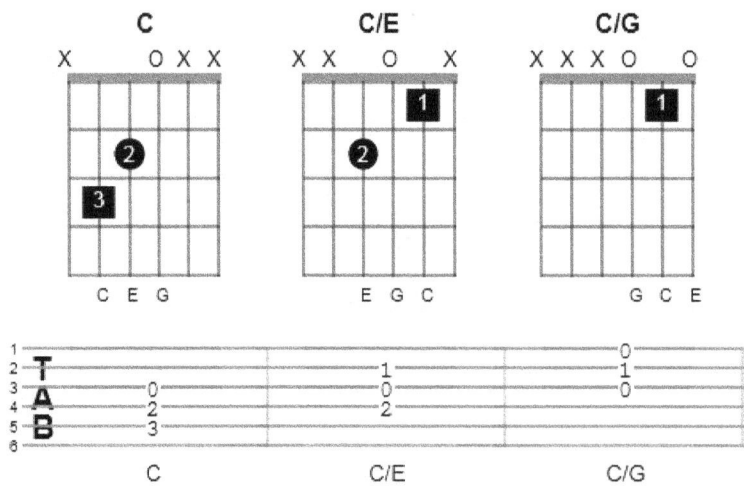

Observe the slash suffixes on two of the chord symbols. Those are explained next.

These lessons do not use many inversions. That could triple the size of the book. But you can experiment with them as you become comfortable and familiar with root position forms.

Slash Chords

When you see a chord symbol with a slash (/) and a note name, such as in the two inversions shown in the previous section, that notation of a *slash chord* specifies that the chord should be played with the slash note on the bottom at the lowest pitch. For example:

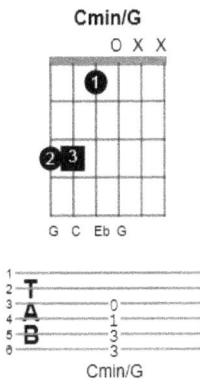

This naming convention serves to say that a note other than the root should be the lowest-pitched note sounded when the chord is played.

There's more to slash chords than that but for now simply play the chord the way you know it. Your playing will not clash with anything that's happening in the tune or that the rest of the band is playing. If it does, you'll hear it and you can do something to fix it then.

Chapter 7, in the discussion titled *Walking Bass Lines*, teaches more about slash chords and why they are important.

Barre

The form shown here includes a *barre* represented by the arc displayed across strings 6 through 1 on fret 5, all of which have finger 1 applied to the fret.

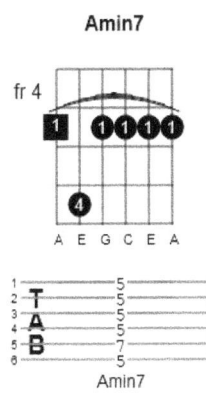

Some writers spell that as *b-a-r*, but "bar" is a synonym for "measure" in musical parlance, and I prefer to avoid ambiguity where possible.

The barre chord just shown is an example of a chord that uses more than four notes, in this case all six strings. It's possible because you play five of the notes with one finger. If you are plucking, you can reduce the note count to four or five by muting strings 1 and/or 2. Those two notes, A and E, are already in the form on strings 5 and 6.

A barre is not always finger 1, it is not always on a lower fret than the other notes in the chord, and it doesn't always stretch across all six strings. For example, look at finger 4 in the Fmaj7 chord shown here.

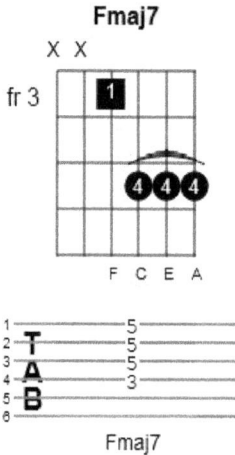

In this chord form, the barre is made by pressing finger 4 across strings 1, 2, and 3 of fret 5 while the root is made with finger 1 on string 4 of fret 3.

Strumming

You can strum the strings up or down either with a pick or your thumb. I strum with my thumb using only down-strokes. A pick provides more volume but I learned by using my thumb back in the days when the nearest music store was thirty miles away and I kept losing the pick. Plus there were no online shopping facilities because there was no online. I came to prefer the quieter sound that my thumb produces. Wes Montgomery uses only his thumb even when picking a melody or improvised line (Chapter 22).

If you strum chords you should be aware of chord forms with unplayed (muted) strings surrounded by played or open strings. You can strum such a chord only if one of your left hand fingers touches the string enough to dampen it without sounding a tone. It sounds a barely audible *thud* instead of a note. Here are examples:

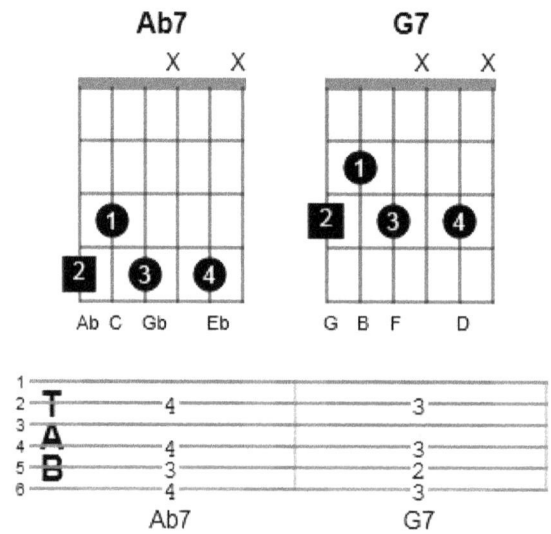

In both chords, string 3 is dampened with the fleshy part of finger 3 or 4, whichever works for you. It wouldn't have to be dampened in the G7 chord, since the open tone of string 3 is the note G, which doesn't conflict harmonically with the G7 chord. But for the form to be transposable (Chapter 6), you dampen it. When you move your hand in that form to the next lower or higher position, the transposition to F#7 or Ab7 works without dissonance.

If you strum, a chord form can use up to six notes because that's how many strings there are. Few chords need six notes, however. Four is usually sufficient to sound the chord. Five can add a fifth note to color the chord (Chapter 9).

Plucking

Some jazz guitarists prefer to use the thumb to push down on only the root note (or the note on the lowest-pitched string) and pull up on the higher-pitched strings at the same time with their index, middle, and ring fingers, using their pinkie only when the chord form calls for a fifth note.

Muted strings do not need to be dampened when you pluck rather than strum. You simply don't pluck the ones that are marked as unplayed in the grid or the tab.

Plucking sounds all the chord's notes at one time, which is a sound some players prefer. It allows you to make the chords sound "short" with space between them when you raise your left fingers off the fretboard after the chord sounds. It keeps the chords from ringing and makes for a solid timekeeper's beat.

Plucking also allows for a stride effect in which the thumb plays the root note by itself and the other fingers pluck the chord on the next beat. Players who are proficient in this technique can walk a bass line with their thumb while they comp (Chapter 21) with their fingers on the higher-pitched, lower-numbered strings.

Rhythm Playing

A rhythm guitarist keeps the chords and time going by strumming or plucking with a strong four-beat (or three if it's a waltz). The guitarist forms the chord on the fretboard and strums or plucks the pertinant strings. After that the player lifts his left fingers from the strings so the chord does not sustain, which presents a quick beat sound, what the theorists call *staccato*. This technique is a reliable time-keeper and lays down the harmonic context as well. For more on this method of playing see Chapter 20 to learn how the great Freddie Green does it.

Chapter 5. Notation

Guitarists who read music use one or more of several formats, called *notation*. Which format you read depends on your training and experience. Many guitarists don't read at all, depending on their ears to tell them what to play. But for you to learn musical technique and methods from a book or read tunes from a chart, we need a way to communicate silently, and that means we must use some kind of notation.

An old joke goes:

How do you get a guitar player to turn down his amp?

Put a sheet of music in front of him.

If you don't read music in any format, if you play strictly "by ear," then you select the strings to strum and the frets to press, leave open, or omit, based on your experience and harmonic intuition. That ability is helpful and even enviable, but you should advance beyond that to one form of music reading or another in order become a versatile jazz player.

Accidentals

We refer to *accidentals* when we discuss notes, in this case the root notes of chords (Chapter 4). An accidental is the sharp (#) or flat (♭) character that you see in key signatures and therefore in chord symbols to the right of the note's name. There is more to accidentals than that, but for now, that's all you need to know.

Standard Notation

The first and most cryptic variation (and, consequentially, the least used) of guitar notation uses standard musical treble clef staff and note representation and is referred to as *piano*, *keyboard*, or *standard* notation as shown here.

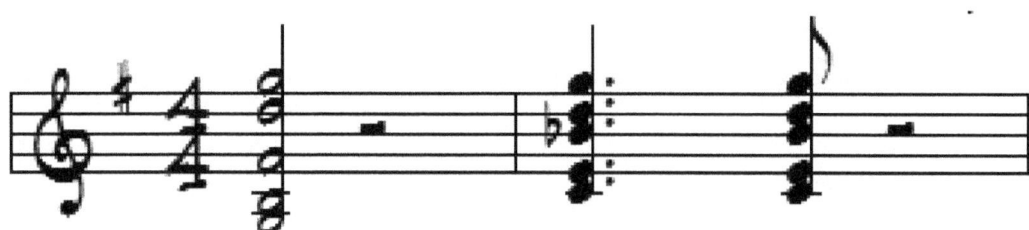

(This format is also often called, simply, *notation*, another ambiguity in musical jargon to add to the confusion.)

You might look at these chords and say, "I don't have that many fingers!" That's okay. Some of the notes could be open strings, Others could be barred (multiple strings on the same fret played with one finger). The guitarist must determine from this notation which notes are open strings, which strings are not played, where on the fretboard to form the chord and which fingers to use. This might work for a classical guitarist, many of whom prefer tablature to standard notation, but the typical jazz guitarist cannot or refuses to read piano notation that fast. The lessons in this book do not use piano notation, but it is shown here so you'll know what it is in case you encounter it in an arrangement.

Grid Notation

The illustration below is a guitar chord *grid*, also called a *diagram*, sometimes called a *frame*.

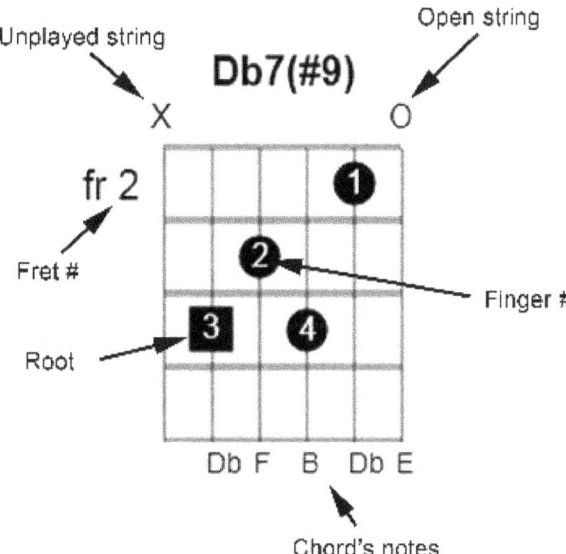

You've probably seen plenty of these. This one depicts a Db7(#9) chord—not to worry; you'll learn about that kind of chord later—and shows many of the features of grid chord representation. It includes digits to tell you which fingers you might use in forming these chords.

The Fret number tells you how far up the fretboard you play the chord. If no fret number is given, you play in the first hand position. In this example, the chord is in the second hand position in that the lowest-pitched fret on the grid is fret 2. This convention allows the grid to depict chord forms up and down the fretboard.

If the frame depicts a chord played in the first position, the top fret line is heavier to represent the nut as shown in this C chord frame.

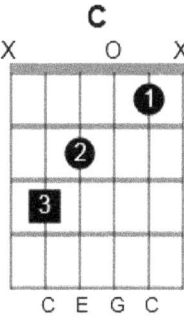

The fingerings shown on the grids in this book are suggestions. Everybody's hands are different and our abilities to stretch and reach change with age. If you find a different fingering configuration to be more comfortable for a particular chord, then by all means use the more comfortable fingering.

Many grid depictions that you see elsewhere do not include finger numbers, leaving that decision to the player. Others place the finger numbers under the grid and do not show the note names. Once again there is no standard.

Tablature

Some guitarists prefer to use *tablature*. Here's the same chord shown as a tab.

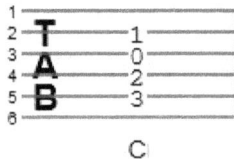

The horizontal lines in a tab are the strings as you would see them with the guitar laying face up on your lap. The digits at the centers of the strings are the fret numbers of the notes in the chord. The zeros are open strings, and unbroken lines represent unplayed strings.

Tabs do not typically depict chord fingerings although there are variations that list the fingers to use in a column under the chord in the tab. But it's usually up to the guitarist to figure out how to finger chords as depicted by tabs.

This book shows its examples as both grids and tabs.

Since tablature by itself does not include sufficient rhythmic notation to show when the chords are to be played in an arrangement, tablature is often paired with standard notation like this:

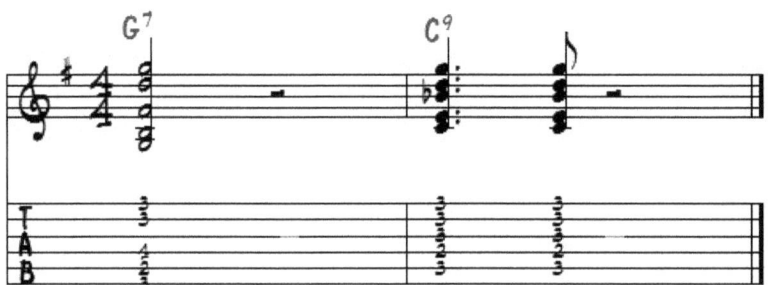

Often the staff representation of the notation uses *rhythmic* notation rather than piano notation as shown here.

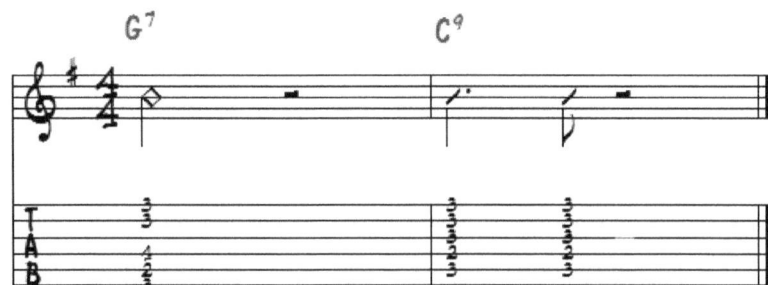

This format tells the guitarist how to play the rhythms. To read such paired notations, you need to understand some of the conventions of lead sheet notation discussed next.

Lead Sheet Notation

The third kind of guitar notation, called *lead sheet* or *fake book* notation, shows the melody in the staff and the chord symbols above the staff just as you would see them at the tops of sheet music, in fake books, lead sheets, and some big band charts. Here's an example.

This notation assumes you already know one or more ways to form the chords and that you'll choose from the ways you know—which frets, which voicing, and so on. The chord symbols shown here are the same ones given at the tops of grids that these lessons use.

Eventually, you'll know all the chords by their symbols and won't need grids or tabs. You'll be playing from lead sheets like the pros do, using only the chord symbols to spell out what chords to play.

Slash Notation

Slash notation is similar to lead sheet notation except that it does not include melody notes. Slashes in the staff tell the guitar player when to strum. This notation is common in big band charts and is similar to and often the same as what the piano and bass players read.

Reading big band charts requires that you understand a few standard notational conventions beyond beat slashes and chord symbols. You must be able to read key signatures, rests, repeats, codas, signs, and endings at a minimum. Dynamics and expressions are important too. They tell you when to play loudly and when to play softly.

Chapter 17 addresses more of the details of this kind of chart. Chapter 19 discusses the reading of big band guitar charts, which often use slash notation.

The example tunes in the PDFs you can download (http://www.alstevens.com/jazzguitar) use slash notation. You'll have to cross-reference the chord symbols with Appendix A until you've put all the chords to memory.

Rhythmic Notation

Chord chart notation often includes selected measures of rhythmic notation when the arranger wants the guitar to match certain rhythmic patterns that the band plays. The following example shows one measure of slash notation and three measures of rhythmic notation.

It takes an understanding of some standard notation—note duration, rests, articulations, repeats, and so on —to correctly read this kind of chart, but this is where you want to be if you are to be a successful jazz guitar accompanist. These are the kinds of charts you'll be reading.

Chapter 18 explains rhythmic notation in more detail.

Nashville Number System

The *Nashville Number System*, or NNS, uses numbers to represent the chord's root name and other symbols to flesh out the chord. The numbers are relative to the major scale notes in the key in which the tune is written where 1 is the tonic, 2, is the second note, 3 is the third, and so on. In the key of C, for example, the digit 1 by itself would represent the C major chord, 2 would represent the D chord, and so on.

The chord's properties are shown as suffixed symbols.

A dominant 7, 9, or 13 is so indicated with those numbers as a suffix.

If the chord's tonic is a sharp or flat relative to the key signature, the note name is prefixed with # or ♭ respectively.

This can be confusing until you get used to it. Hopefully, you won't have to.

Here are the changes to *After You've Gone* in NNS notation

$4^6 . 4^\Delta . | 4^{-6} . \flat 7^7 . | 1^\Delta \ldots | 6^7 \ldots$
$2^7 \ldots | 5^7 \ldots | 1^6 \ldots | \ldots 1^{+7}$
$4^6 . 4^\Delta . | 4^{-6} . \flat 7^7 . | 1^\Delta \ldots | 6^7 \ldots$
$2^{-7} . 6^7 . | 2^{-7} . 4^{-6} \flat 7^7 | 1^6 . 3^7 . | 6^{-7} . 1^{o7} .$
$1^6 \ldots | 5^7 \ldots | 1^6 . 2^{-7} . | 1^{o7} . 1^6 \, 1^{+7}$

The vertical lines represent measure dividers. The dots represent beats on which the current chord is strummed. If you were playing in the key of C, for example, the first chord would be F6. The 4 represents the 4th note of the C scale, which is F.

The chord symbols prefixed with the ♭ symbol are flatted note chords. Sharped note chords would have the # prefix.

The small superscript digit suffixes are the chords' interval numbers (Chapter 4). For example, the ♭7^7 chord is B♭7. The plus (+) character is an augmented chord and the minus (-) character is a minor chord. Delta (Δ) means major 7, and a superscript lowercase o (°) means diminished.

These characters are the same as the ones that some copyists use in standard notation (Chapter 5).

You can work out the other chords in the chart based on that method if you wish.

The last two measures show changes that resolve back to the beginning. After the final chorus, you'd play the C6 chord and then an appropriate ending (Chapter 15) to which everybody agrees.

The advantage to NNS is that the player does not have to transpose a chart if a singer, for example, wants it in a key other than the original. The same chart applies to all key signatures. A disadvantage is that the player must know which notes are represented by which numbers in the key in which the tune is being played. In other words, you have to know the notes in the key signature's major scale (Chapter 8).

There is more to NNS. It includes rhythmic idioms, for example. As a jazz player, you might or might not be expected to read charts notated with NNS. Entire books have been written on the subject. If you need to know about it, a search of Amazon and Wikipedia serves up many references.

Internet Notation

Internet notation is relatively new, so new that I had to come up with a name for it. There is no standard, so you'll see many variations on how it is written.

Internet notation came to be when musicians needed to swap chord changes in e-mail and online discussion forums. They had only the text characters of their keyboards with which to convey chord changes, so they formed chord symbols, beats and barlines with letters, numbers and special characters from the ASCII character set, the standard encoding system with which most personal computers encode conversational exchanges between English-speaking human beings. Here are the changes for *After You've Gone* written out in Internet notation in the key of C.

F / Fmaj7 / | Fmin6 / Bb7 / | Cmaj7 / / / | A7 / / / |

D7 / / / | G7 / / / | C6 / / / | / / / Caug7 |

F / Fmaj7 / | Fmin6 / Bb7 / | Cmaj7 / / / | A7 / / / |

Dmin7 / A7 / | Dmin7 / Fmin6 Bb7 | C6 / E7 / | Amin7 / Cdim7 / |

C6 / / / |G7 / / / | C6 / Dmin7 / | Cdim7 / C6 Caug7 |

The slashes are beats that repeat the prior chord kind of like slash notation. The vertical lines (|) are barlines.

Summary

Other notation conventions exist. A variety of NNS uses Roman numerals instead of Arabic numerals, using upper and lower case to designate major and minor chords. *ABC Notation* uses the ASCII character set to encode melodic lines. *MusicXML* is a code language derived from XML, which is used to encode documents and web pages.

You could make a career of knowing all the different ways musicians and music publishers notate music.

Do that if it interests you, but we'll use mostly grids and tabs to show how to play the chords in these lessons, and we'll use mostly slash notation to illustrate the longer sequences of chords you've already learned. Study Part V in this book to see how all this comes together on paper both from the viewpoint of the fake book reader and the guitarist in big bands.

Chapter 6. Transposable Forms

Up to now we've been learning chord forms, some of which have fixed positions on the fretboard and cannot be used in other fret positions because they depend on open strings. This chapter addresses what I call the *transposable* chord form, which is where a common configuration of finger positions works up and down the fretboard to make like-sounding chords with different roots.

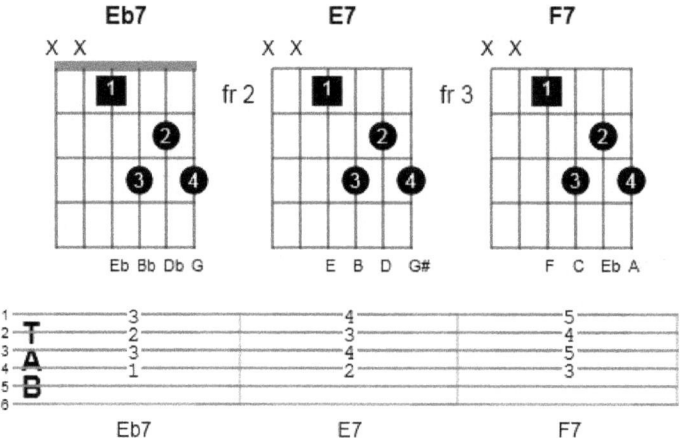

In this example, we are using the same form to sound three dominant 7 chords by moving our left hand up the fretboard one position as indicated in these grids by the fret number to the left of the lowest fret in the grid. You can continue moving your left hand until you run out of frets.

Transposables with Open Strings

There is, however, one set of chord forms with open strings that can be transposed by changing positions. These are forms in which the open strings are within two frets of the fingered frets and the distance between fingered and open frets is fewer than four notes. With these forms, you can move your hand to the next higher position and use your index finger as a barre to simulate the nut much as a capo would do.

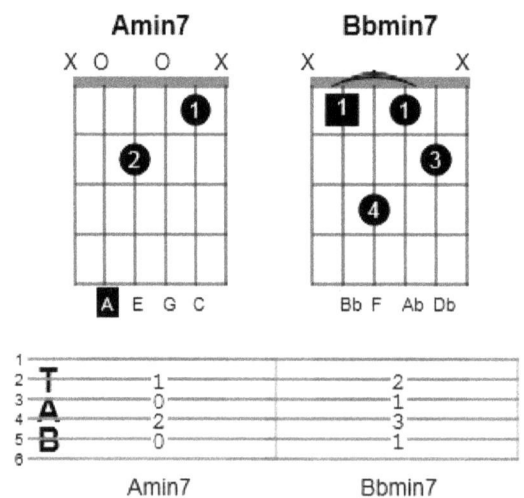

Even though the fingering changes, the form is still the same. You can then proceed up the fretboard with the barred form to make chords with successively and chromatically higher roots.

Observe that the B♭min7 chord in the first position is transposable up the fretboard without your having to change the chord form. As you move your hand upward, the chord becomes Bmin7, Cmin7, D♭min7, and so on.

That chord form is a barre chord that uses the index finger to cover strings 1 through 5. All such barre chords are transposable. Once you've learned the form, you need only know where the root note is that you want for the corresponding chord type, and you know how to play the chord.

If only one string is open, it doesn't have to be barred when you transpose it. For example:

Again, the E♭min7 chord is transposable up the fretboard, giving you Emin7, Fmin7, F#min7, and so on.

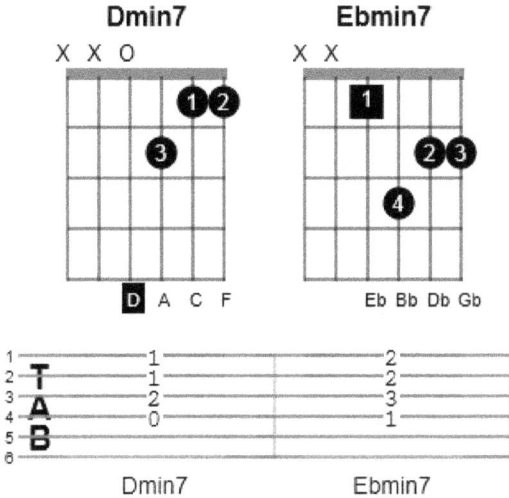

A Tradition

Lest you think I am letting you in on some deep secret, know this: Transposable forms are not strangers to experienced guitarists. If you are a fledgling guitarist you probably watch the guitar player's left hand on television, on YouTube, and in live performances to see what he or she is doing, to see if you can recognize the chords being played. You usually see a lot of barre chords with the player's index finger crossing the fretboard. Those are transposable chords. The player accompanying the singer or soloist knows which tonal center is in effect (Chapter 10) and typically sticks to two or three common forms, moving the left hand up and down the fretboard to land on the chord of choice.

Not all your chords absolutely need to be transposable. You have many chords with open strings at your disposal. Choose the chord that's most convenient to reach at the time and that you can easily play.

Chapter 7. Other Essential Chords

This chapter discusses several chords you will encounter in jazz and big band arrangements. They include the diminished, half diminished, augmented, suspended chords, and chords with flatted 5ths and sharped and flatted 9ths. It sounds like a lot, but you will see that most of them don't get used nearly as often as the old reliable major, minor 7 and dominant 7 chords.

Diminished

A diminished chord contains three or four notes with each note being the minor 3rd of the note that precedes it.

C diminished would consist of the notes, C, E♭, G♭, and, optionally, A.

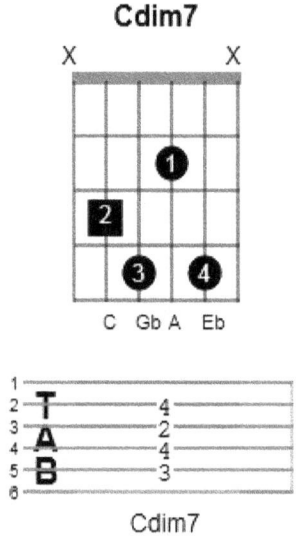

Observe that the notes are not played in the same sequence that we describe the chord. The chord does not arpeggiate up the scale exactly the way it would on a keyboard. That is just the nature of note orientation on a fretboard. You could do it if you had monster hands, but it wouldn't fit on a grid.

There are two kinds of diminished chords. The symbol for one is named *dim* and the other is named *dim7*. The chord shown above is a diminished 7. The diminished chord has three notes. The diminished 7 chord has four notes. We'll discuss only the diminished 7 chord because wherever you see a chord symbol with the suffix *dim*, the diminished 7 chord will fit. Theory scholars might argue with that statement, but in decades of big band and combo playing, I've never found it to be otherwise.

There are only three diminished 7 chords. That's right, only three. There are twelve notes, and each note can be the root of a diminished chord, but here's how it works:

A diminished 7 chord is a root and three notes, each note three half steps above the previous one. So, as we saw above, C diminished 7 contains these notes:

C, E♭, G♭, and A

Now, consider the E♭dim7 chord. It's notes are:

E♭, G♭, A, and C

Right away you notice that E♭dim7 contains the same notes as Cdim7 only in a different inversion.

Now look at G♭dim7 and Adim7, which contain these notes:

G♭, A, C, E♭

A, C, E♭, G♭

Here are all four diminished 7 chords from the C, E♭, G♭, A family:

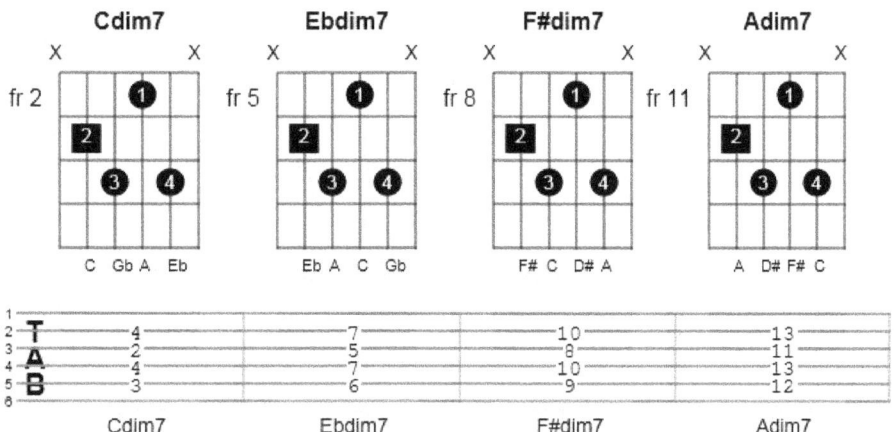

Look at the notes at the bottoms of the grids. They're all the same notes (albeit different octaves) in different orders. And the chords are all interchangeable. Wherever one of them is called for on a chart, you can play any of the others.

Don't forget that G♭ and E♭ are also F♯ and D♯ respectively.

Now consider these same four diminished 7 chords, which use a different common form but with their roots on string 4 instead of string 5:

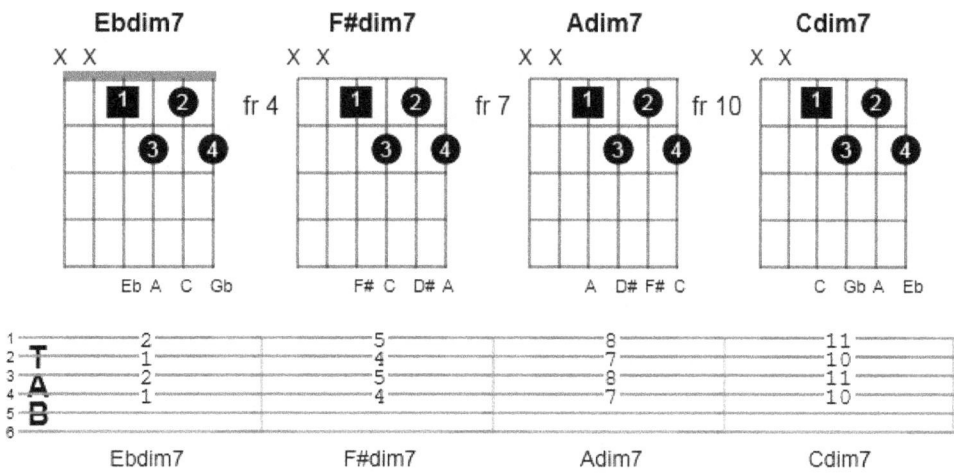

Same chord, different inversions, which means the roots are not necessarily the lowest-pitched note in the form. You can play all four diminished 7 chords we just showed by using the same form in the same fret position. That makes it easy, because there's just one form to remember. There are other forms, and we'll get into them soon, but the point is, if a chord symbol on a chart is one of those four diminished chords, the one form and fret position will work.

Now, what about the other two diminished 7 chords? Here they are:

Fdim7 contains these notes:

F, A♭, B, D,

which are the same notes as in A♭dim7, Bdim7, and Ddim7, which can all be played with the same form as shown here:

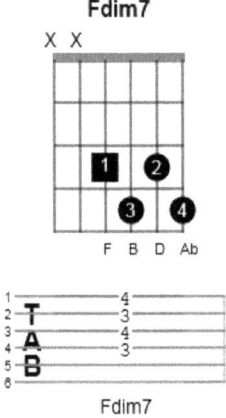

Gdim7 contains these notes:

G, B♭, D♭, E,

which are the same notes as in B♭dim7, D♭dim7, and Edim7, which can all be played with the same form as shown here:

The grids shown so far for the diminished 7 chords are transposable. I've shown them with the named root on string 4 and the other three notes on strings 3, 2, and 1.

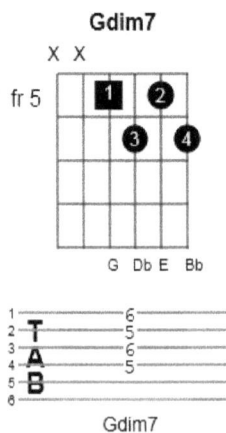

Here are the diminished 7 chords with the root on string 6. These forms are transposable too.

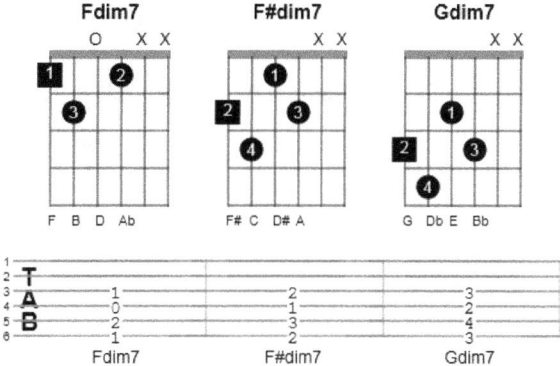

You would use these voicings when you need a lower-pitched sound to your chord. If you move to the next higher position, you are playing an Ab dim7, which has the same four notes as and can be played in place of the Fdim7 as a first inversion.

When No Substitution Will Do

There are places where only the diminished 7 chord as written (or one of its inversions) will work. You should not substitute something else. An example is in the last eight measures of Gershwin's *S'Wonderful*.

> *In the 1980s, I was in Blues Alley, a club in Washington DC, listening to jazz vocalist, Anita O'Day, singing S'Wonderful in the key of G. When she hit the lyric, "s'marvelous..." at the end, which calls for a Gdim7 chord, the pianist played instead an A7 chord, which has some of the same notes but without that distinctive diminished sound. After a couple choruses like that, Ms. O'Day, clearly irritated at the pianist's inept interpretation of the song, sang these lyrics for those four measures: "S'Wonderful, G-dim-in-ished sev-en..." arpeggiating the chord downward as she sang its name.*
>
> *He didn't get it right on the out chorus either.*

Half Diminished (min7b5)

The half-diminished chord provides a nice change when used to resolve to a dominant 7 or augmented 7 chord. It is essentially a min7 chord with its 5th flatted. The flatted fifth note makes a nice resolution downward a half tone to the root of the chord being resolved to, which relates the resolution to both the usual ii7-I and the tritone substitution (Chapter 16).

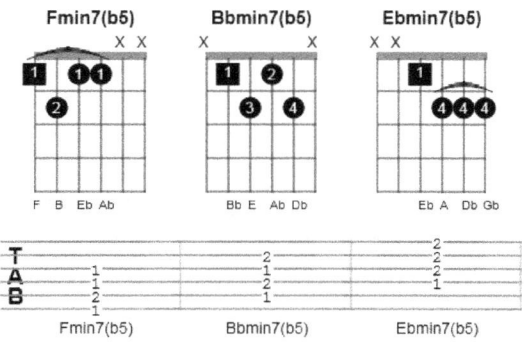

A close look reveals that min7(b5) chords are inversions of the min6 chords of their 3rd. For example, Dmin7(b5) has the same notes as Fmin6 as shown here:

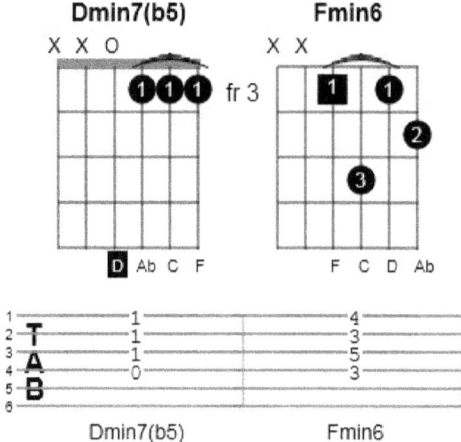

Old sheet music for popular songs used to substitute the chord symbols and grids of min6 chord for the min7(b5) chord. When reading those old sheet music tunes from my mother's piano bench, I'd see Dmin6 resolving to E7, for example, but the simple two-clef piano arrangement would show a B as the lowest bass clef note. When I learned more about theory, I opined that the old substitutions were because the publishers understood that typical amateur guitar and ukulele players would be more likely to recognize and play the minor 6 chord.

Augmented

The augmented chord can be named aug, +, or +5. For example, you might see the C augmented chord symbol spelled Caug. C+, or C+5. It's purpose is to provide a major chord when the melody note wants to be one half tone up from the major chord's 5th.

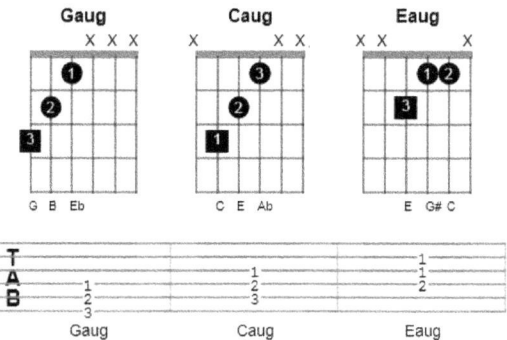

For example, in *Poor Butterfly* the Caug in measure 5 reflects a C chord with G#/Ab as the melody note.

The Caug could also be Caug7 (discussed next) because it resolves to F9.

There are only four augmented chords if you consider the inversions. The three notes in an augmented chord are complementary. Gaug is G, B and Eb. B augmented is B, Eb and G. Ebaug is Eb, G and B.

Augmented 7

This chord is named *augmented 7* which might lead you to believe the 7th is augmented. It isn't, of course. It's a dominant 7 chord with the 5th augmented just as in an augmented chord.

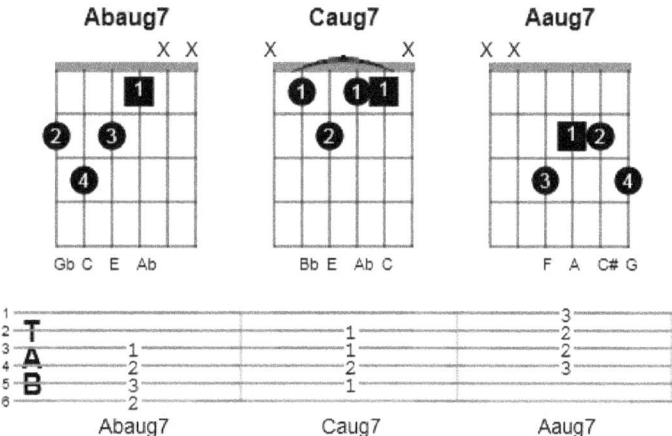

The augmented 7 chord supports resolving to the next chord in the cycle with the tonic's blue minor 3rd in the melody. It is also used in minor keys in place of the usual dominant 7 to resolve to the minor tonic chord. The augmented 5th of the aug7 chord is also the minor 3rd of the tonic chord.

Suspended

A suspended chord is typically a dominant 7 chord with the 3rd left out and the root of the next expected chord substituted for the 3rd. That note is one half-tone above the 3rd.

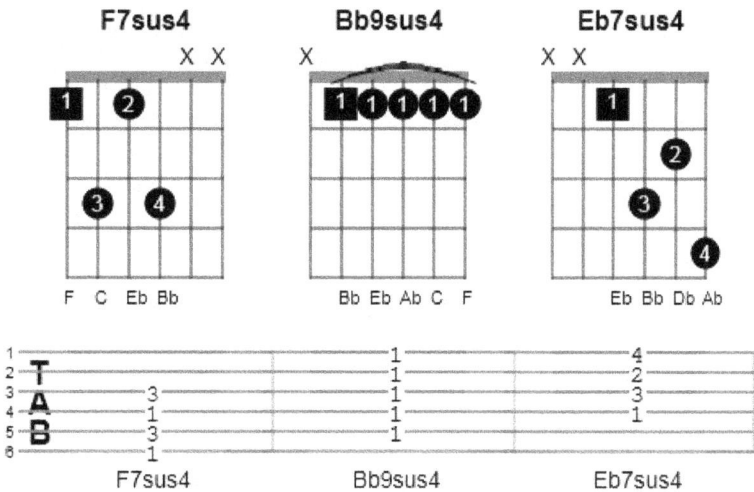

Observe in the F7sus4 chord that a B♭ is where you'd normally expect an A. That B♭ is what provides the suspended sound of the chord.

You would use a suspended chord, for example, when the melody note is the root of the I chord of the current tonal center (Chapter 10) while the chord is the V7. Looking at a fragment of the old standard, *Blue Moon* we find three incidents of a B♭7sus chord. Here's the first of them.

The B♭7sus chord in measure 6 is suspended because the melody note throughout its duration is an E♭. But the tune hasn't fully resolved to the E♭ chord in measure 7, so the suspended chord suspends the E♭ note as part of the B♭7sus chord.

Pull up a recording of *Blue Moon* on YouTube to hear an example of this usage.

Flatted Fifth (♭5)

The flatted fifth is believed to be the Holy Grail for be-bop jazz and beyond. But you'll find it in classical music going back centuries. In jazz, a flatted fifth chord is usually called for when the melody note is the flatted fifth of the chord. Here are three transposable forms with the roots on strings 6, 5, and 4.

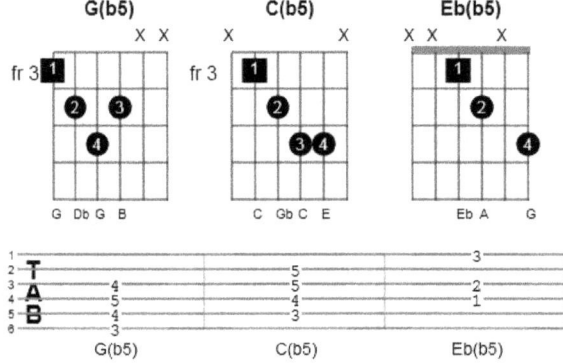

The first two flatted fifth chord forms repeat the root note on another string. If you're plucking, you can leave the redundant root out. Or, if strumming, mute the extra note. String 2 on the rightmost form must be muted. No note within reach fits with the chord.

Sharp Eleven (♯11)

Sharp eleven is a variation of the flatted fifth but one that includes both the unflatted fifth and the dominant 7 notes. It serves as an alternative way to resolve to the chord coming up. The flatted fifth harmonically resolves a half-tone downward and the root resolves up to the tonic chord next in the harmonic cycle.

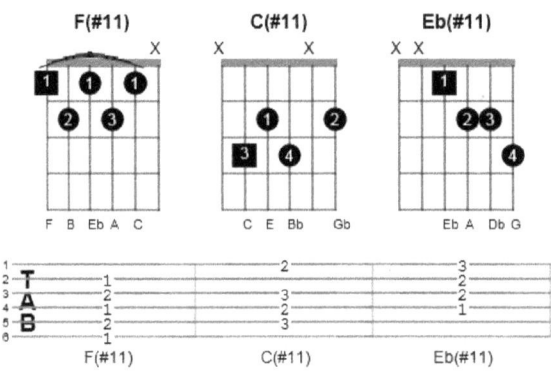

To illustrate, F7, the dominant 7 part of the F(♯11) chord naturally resolves up to B♭. B, the sharp 11 (flat 5) part of the F(♯11) resolves a half tone downward to the B♭.

Sharp Nine (♯9)

Sharp nine adds a bluesy feeling to a dominant 7 chord. It adds the tonic's primary blues note, the minor third, to its major chord. Chapter 22 discusses blue notes.

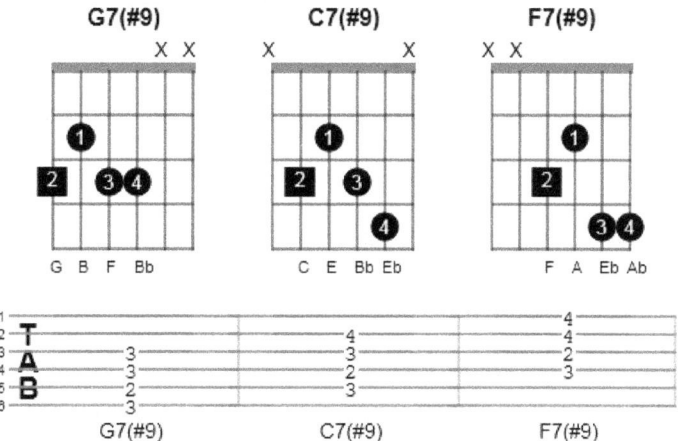

Remember, nine is seven plus two. For the sharp nine to work, the 3rd must be included in the chord. Otherwise, the shape nine which is also a flatted third gives the chord a minor sound. The sharp nine is best played with that note at the highest position in the form. It needs distance from the major third to avoid the sound of dissonance.

Flat Nine (♭9)

A flat nine chord is a dominant 7 chord with a flatted ninth note added at the top. It provides a modern color to the chord and is often needed when the melody calls for that note.

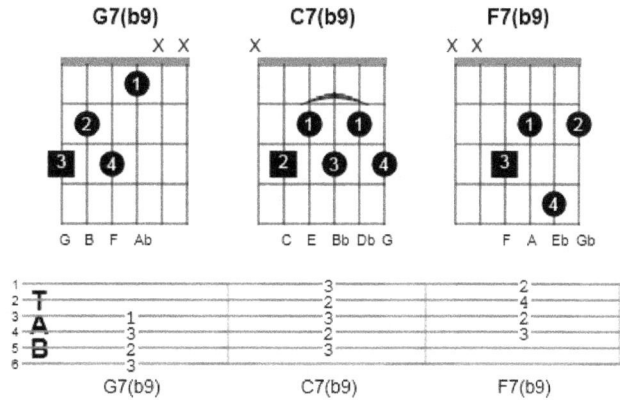

Just like the sharp nine, the flatted ninth note needs to be at the top of the chord to maintain distance from the root note. A flatted ninth is the same note that is one-half step above the root, and putting them too close together makes for dissonance.

A diminished 7 chord can also be used where a flat nine chord is called for. Figuring out which diminished chord to substitute for which flat nine can be tricky. Consider this example:

A C7(♭9) chord consists of the notes C, E, G, B♭, and D♭. That's more fingers than you have, so unless you use an open string for the E or G, something has to be left out. And not all flat nine chord forms will have open strings. If you omit the flatted nine note, D♭ in this case, you're playing a basic C7, which does not provide the color of the chord that was called for. It might even seem to clash with a melody note. But if you omit the root (C in this case), you're left with E, G, B♭, and D♭, which happens to also be the E diminished 7 chord. These grids show both chords side by side. Observe the note names under the grids.

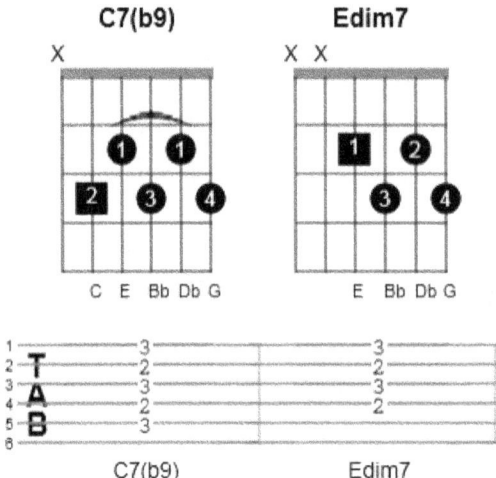

You can also substitute any of the three other inversions of the E diminished 7 chord.

To remember which chord to substitute, use the root of the flat nine chord and play the diminished 7 chord with a root one half tone higher. than that of the flat nine chord. In this case, the C7(♭9) chord is played as a D♭dim7 chord or, as shown above, one of its inversions because D♭ is pitched a half tone above C.

Alternate (Alt)

You'll occasionally see a chord with the *alt* quality. It means the arranger wants to hear a chord with a flatted 9th, a sharped 9th, a flatted 5th, and maybe even an augmented (sharped) 5th. In other words, almost all the notes except the root are altered. That's advanced modern jazz theory, more than you should be learning now, but here's a shortcut, a way to cheat.

When the score calls for an altered chord, play the major 7th for the next higher chord a half step up. For example, if you see Calt, play D♭maj7. It won't be right according to strict musical theory, but it will sound right and nobody will yell at you for playing the wrong chord.

Walking Bass Lines

Slash chords (Chapter 4) are often used to define a so-called *walking* bass line where the bottom is expected to provide an ascending or descending line that includes notes other than the roots of their corresponding chords.

If there's a bass player, don't worry about the bottom notes of slash chords. Just play the chord the way you know it; the bass player has your bottom. But if it's just you—if, for example, you're accompanying a vocalist with no other rhythm instruments—then you should play the bass line as the bottom-most note in each of the first four chords something like this:

Walkup

Here is where slash chords can affect how you form a chord. Consider this set of changes which includes one inversion:

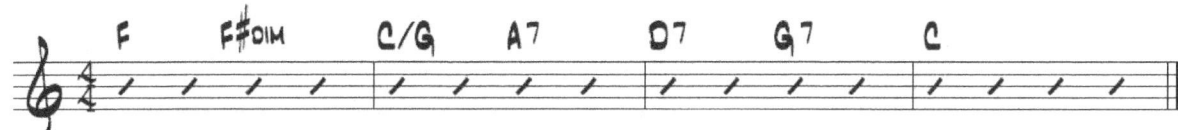

You might have a favorite form for the diminished chord with the bottom note being one of its four notes as explained above. But the changes tell you something different.

These could be the changes to the last four measures of a tune in C or they could be an ending or a tag (Chapter 15). The clue about what bottom notes to play is seen in the slash chord, C/G, in the second measure. That tells you (or the bass player) that the bass note for that chord is G and the bass line for the first two measures in the passage should be:

F, F♯, G, A...

...the first three notes of which are an ascending chromatic line. Nothing about the notation demands that. It's simply a convention that jazz players recognize.

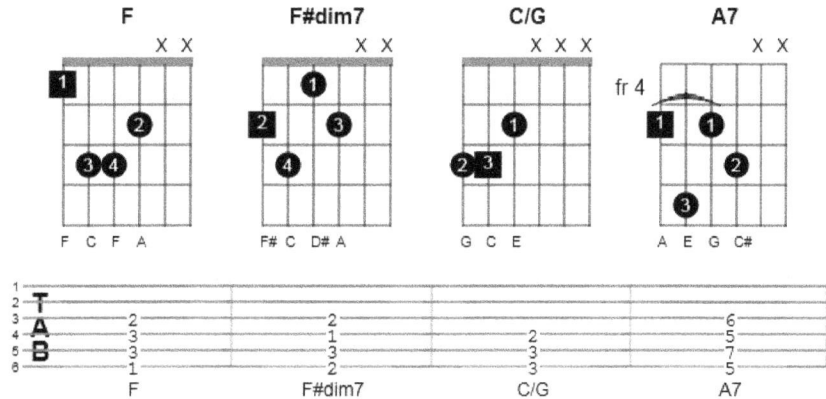

If you're playing an arrangement of a band chart, the arranger has probably written notes on the bass clef staff for the bass player instead of or in addition to chord symbols. In that case, just play the chords the way you know them without worrying about walking.

Walkdown

Sometimes you'll see a similar pattern where the bass notes define a descending scale, also known as a *walkdown*, shown here with a bass line on string 4 walking chromatically from F to D and resolving from Fmin7 to B♭7.

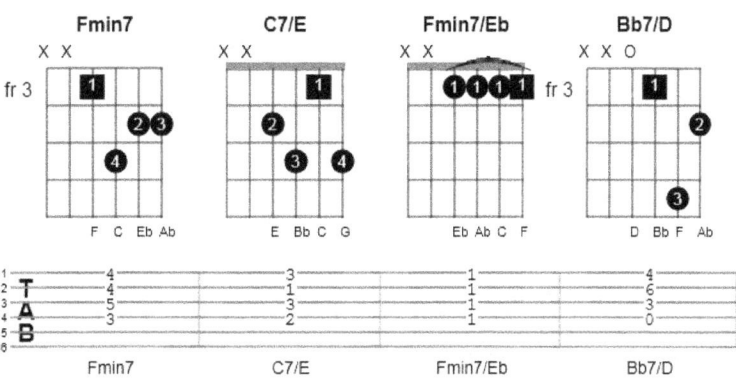

The second chord could also be Fmin(maj7)/E as long as you and the piano player agree. I wouldn't play the fourth chord with that particular form only because it's too much of a stretch for me and more so if I try to move the form up the fretboard and press the corresponding note on string 4.

These walking patterns might suggest that you need to learn every inversion of every chord with the bottom on every string in order to accommodate any possible walking bass line. I wouldn't worry about that. You don't see it often enough for it to matter whether you get it absolutely correct. If such a chord shows up in an arrangement that you'll be playing frequently and there's no bass player, then work out how to form an inversion of the chord with the correct bottom note. Otherwise, just play the chord.

If all this seems like a lot of complexity to put inside your head, don't worry. With time and experience—lots of time and lots of experience—these concepts become second nature. Simply learn tunes that use these chords and, as with everything related to playing music, let their sounds and touch find their way into your harmonic and muscle memories.

PART III. Theory

Part III is about the dreaded subject, m*usic theory.* If you already know formal music theory at an advanced level, you might want to skip to Part IV. But I urge you to scan Part III just so you'll know we're on the same page when some terms come into play later in the lessons.

You can play chords without knowing any of what Part III teaches. You can simply read the chord symbols from charts and plug happily away. That's well and good if all your playing is from charts. But if you want to jam when someone names a tune and a key and counts it off, a tune you've heard but have no chart for, you need to know a touch of theory. You need to know not only how to form the next chord based on its symbol on a sheet of paper; you need to know which chord is expected next based on the harmonic context in which you *hear* the chord.

You need to be able to play "by ear." And for most musicians, ear playing requires an understanding of basic music theory.

But, your choice. If you want only to read charts or play tunes by ear that employ the usual three or four chords, then by all means skip to Part IV. But you'll be missing out on a lot.

Chapter 8. Theory 101

If this chapter is your introduction to musical theory, you might come to it with some hesitation. Don't be intimidated by the technical jargon you hear from theorists and pedants. You won't have to learn all that stuff in these lessons, and you won't have to take any tests. The measure of what you've learned is found in what you play. And one cardinal rule overrides all others:

If it sounds right, it's right.

Octaves

If you pluck string 2, fret 1 followed by string 5, fret 3, you have played two Cs an *octave* apart. String 4, fret 5 and string 6, fret 8 sound the same two notes.

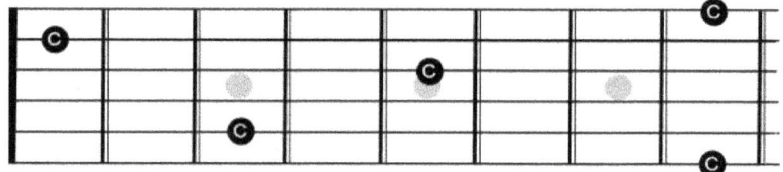

The second note of each pair sounds like the first note an octave lower.

What about that stray C in the upper right corner on string 1, fret 8? It has no partner. Well, yes it does, but the partner is too far off the diagram to show here. But that C shows you something important. On every fret, strings 1 and 6 sound the same note two octaves apart. Knowing that comes in handy when we form barre chords (Chapter 4).

Intervals

An interval is the distance in tones between two notes. Adjacent notes are said to be a *half tone* away from each other. C is a half tone up from B, which is a half tone up from B♭, and so on. There are twelve half-tone intervals between the notes in an octave, and if you play them in succession in either direction, up or down, you are playing what is called the *chromatic* scale. And, no matter where you start playing an ascending chromatic scale the note immediately after the twelfth note, the thirteenth note, of course, is an octave above the first one.

The octave is an *interval.* It is said to consist of a span of eight tones, thus its name, but it really spans twelve *half tones.* When you try to do the math, it gets confusing. So don't try to do the math.

Half Tones

A *half tone* is the next note up or down for the same string on the fretboard. Begin at any fret on string 6 and play the half tone notes one after the other in ascending order. When you reach at note that can be continued on the next higher string, move your hand up and across and continue playing as this fretboard illustration shows.

teach yourself Rhythm Jazz Guitar, *a player's guide* – Al Stevens

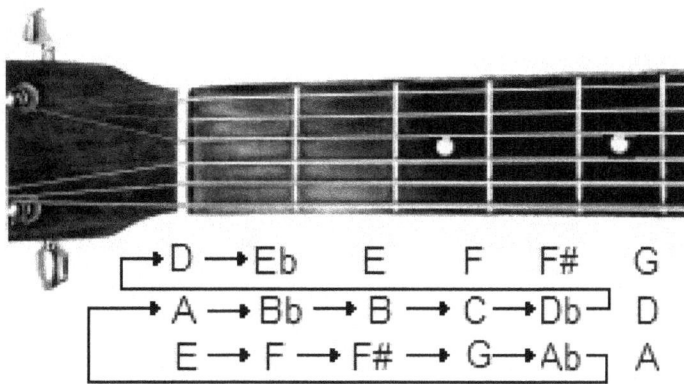

After you've played the twelfth tone and then play the next one—the E on string 4 in this example—you've completed an octave of half tones, which is also an octave of the chromatic scale. Some of these tones are *naturals* (no accidentals) and others are *sharps* and/or *flats* (accidentals).

You can play this pattern beginning with any fret within reasonable reach. The point is to understand what half-tone intervals are, how they relate to one another, and where they are on the fretboard.

Scales

Students of musical instruments are encouraged to practice *scales* repetitively until they can play them by memory. But few teachers ever explain why you should practice scales other than to say that scales improve your technique. That's true, of course, but there are other reasons to know scales when you improvise. For now, an understanding of scales and the relationships between their notes is essential to a full understanding of music theory.

But you don't have to practice scales for these lessons. It wouldn't hurt you to do so, but it isn't mandatory. You need to understand scales and know the notes that comprise them, but you don't have to play them proficiently. Music teachers across the land are flinging their metronomes at me right now, but I hold my ground. To play proficient chordal accompaniment on the guitar, you do not need to have developed a proficiency with scales. Improvisation (Chapter 22), however, is a different matter.

A piano keyboard represents the perfect depiction of scales. Each white note is a natural and each black note is a flat or sharp.

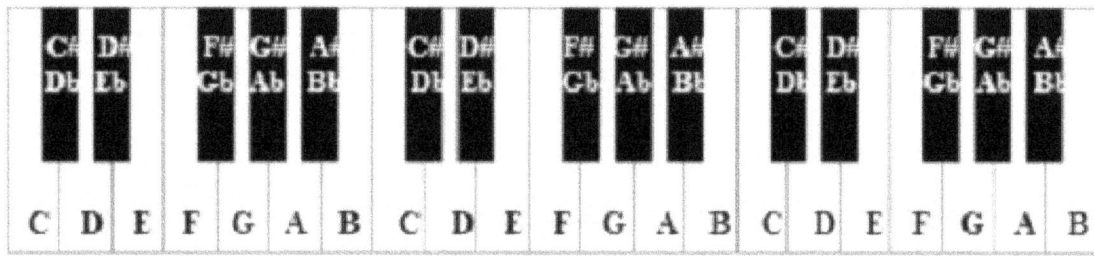

Actually, every black note is a flat *and* a sharp as the picture shows, and some white notes are also flats or sharps. B is C♭, C is B♯, E is F♭, and F is E♯. Confused? Don't worry about it. You rarely run into these note names in your reading experiences unless you're playing classical music, in which case you're already way past this discussion.

teach yourself Rhythm Jazz Guitar, *a player's guide* – Al Stevens

Keyboard notes played in succession—when you play the next key adjacent to the current one—are also the chromatic scale beginning on whichever note you started with and ending wherever you wish.

A scale is a series of intervals measured in whole and half tones. Consider the C major scale, for example.

C, D, E, F, G, A, B

It's almost the alphabet except that it begins on C and jumps back to A after the G. But count the letters. C is the first, D is the second, and so on. That's why when musicians refer to the fourth in the C scale, for example, they are referring to the note F. It's the fourth note in the scale.

These numbers, fourth and fifth in this case, are intervals, and they are also crucial to an understanding of harmonic theory. This is why you need to understand scales. When you hear mention of the third, fifth, seventh, whatever, you need to know which note that is in the current chord under discussion. In a C major scale, the third is E. In E♭, the third is G, in F, the third is A, and so on.

To the uninitiated, the notes in a major scale are just letters. But think of the tune we all learned from *The Sound of Music*, which uses other names for the notes in a major scale.

Do, re, mi, fa, sol, la, ti, do.

These names, called collectively, *solfeggio*, can apply to any major scale. It just depends on which note you begin and end with. If you are in the key of C, *do* at the beginning is C, and *do* at the end is C an octave above the first one.

If that seems too simple, it isn't. The C to B scale consists of all natural notes, which isn't obvious on the fretboard but is on the keyboard. Consider the E♭ major scale:

E♭, F, G, A♭, B♭, C, D

Some of these notes, the first one included, have accidentals (flats in this case).

The first note in the scale is called the *tonic*. From there, a major scale moves upward in tonal intervals like this:

Tonic, whole step, whole step, half step, whole step, whole step, whole step, half step.

That last half step lands on the tonic note an octave higher than the original.

In theoretical jargon, the fourth note is the *subdominant*, and the fifth note is the *dominant*.

The C *minor* scale is formed with these intervals:

C, D, E♭, F, G, A♭, B♭, C

There's more to scales than this section describes, but it's enough for a general discussion of theory.

I will, however, ease your apprehension about putting to memory all the notes in all the scales. Instead of remembering the component notes of, for example, the minor chord of a specified tonic, you will learn how to play that chord. If the music sheet says, for example, E♭7, you will know one of three ways to form that chord on the fretboard and which strings to strum or pluck. That's a lot of things to remember, but more than some abstract recollection of note names and finger placement is involved. With practice you will learn which chord to play because of how it sounds.

Memory is something you remember. You remember things long term that you drum into your memory repetitively. The more often you play a chord in a particular harmonic context, the more deeply you burn it into your harmonic memory and your muscle memory. When it comes to you on its own without your having to think about it, you have that chord nailed. On to the next chord.

The same thing applies to every possible sequence of chord changes. Eventually you will play all of them so often they will become second nature.

Playing by ear requires that you learn music starting at the lowest level of abstraction and working your way up. Those levels are, starting at the lowest:

Note, chord, chord changes, tune.

Looking at the levels top down, it should be obvious that tunes are groups of changes, which are groups of chords, which are groups of notes.

Chord Resolutions

Chapter 4 taught you about the major, minor, dominant 7 and minor 7 chords. Now we'll put those chords into a harmonic context. We have to use them and others like them to play tunes. There are, of course, more major chords, more minor chords and more dominant 7 chords than Chapter 4 showed you, and their grid forms can be different. But we're at a good start. Next we must address how the chords *resolve* to one another.

An old folk tale helps to explain harmonic resolution.

In the story, Mozart, according to some versions, and Chopin, according to others, lies in bed trying to get some rest. Some versions put the composer on his deathbed to dramatize and thus emphasize the point of the story.

The story goes as follows:

> *While Mozart/Chopin is trying to fall asleep, someone downstairs is at the piano playing a tune. The pianist takes the piece up to the next to the last chord and then for one reason or another gets up from the piano without completing it and walks away.*
>
> *The composer, unable to sleep while the incomplete tune remains unresolved, leaves his bed, rushes to the piano, and plays the last chord, after which he returns to bed and goes to sleep.*

Why would he do that? To *resolve* the incomplete harmonic sequence that's been left unspoken, or hanging. To *hear* the ending. To finish it.

That's what chord resolution is. The listener hears a melody or some changes and expects to hear them resolve with a very specific sound, with the note or chord that completes the passage.

Of course, it's difficult to explain in words what something sounds like. But we can try. Chord changes that you'd expect to resolve to a tonic, go somewhere else, perhaps to another set of changes. But eventually there should be a closing resolution, and you hear what you expect to hear.

There is a way to understand resolution, a way that I can describe by using something with which everyone is familiar.

> **Exercise:** Sing the last part of *Happy Birthday* to yourself. Start with "Happy Birthday, dear..." but don't sing the final note. Leave that note hanging. Ask anyone within earshot to sing what they expect to hear. They'll sing, "you" and unless they are tone deaf, it will be your resolved note.

Now consider these changes, which fit with the end of *Happy Birthday* in G. The lead-in "Happy" does not have a chord here. Start with "Birthday, dear..." It's in 3/4 time, so the first two chords take three beats each, the third takes two, the fourth takes one, and the last chord takes three.

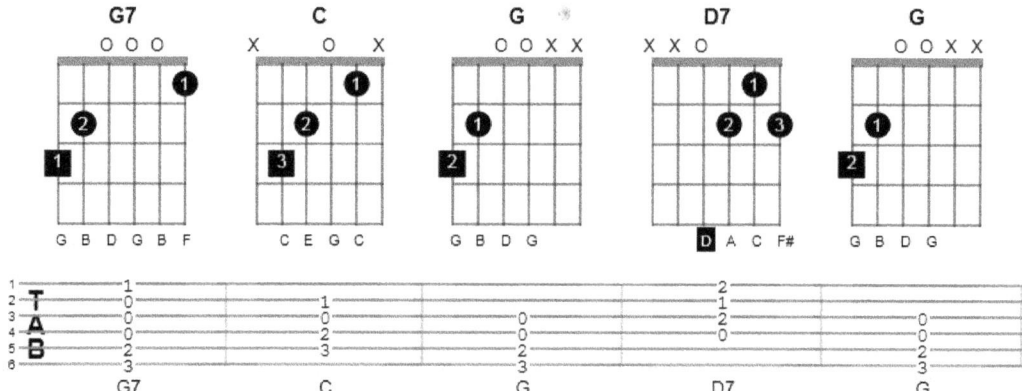

That last chord, the G, is your resolved chord. The D7 makes you expect to hear the G chord played. Leave it out, and Chopin and Mozart will fall over each other, running downstairs.

Resolution also occurs in places in the tune other than at the end. The first chord, the G7, in the example above resolves to the C that follows it.

The resolving chord symbol in a passage is usually named with the note that ends the passage. So, if you are in the key of G, the last note of the tune's melody is usually G because that's what the listener expects to hear. And the last chord is probably G major. If the tune is in G minor, the last melody note is G and the last chord is G minor.

There are many exceptions to this simple rule, all of which could confuse you at this point, so we won't delve into them. Let's keep it simple for now.

The Cycle/Circle of Fifths/Fourths

What makes one chord suggest the next chord in sequence? What elements in a chord generate the tension that wants to be resolved by the next one? And which second chord does the first chord suggest?

You've probably seen variations on this illustration in other works about musical theory. Harmonic resolution involves *tension* in the tune's harmonic context which must be resolved, usually by a chord from the counter-clockwise adjacent note in the circle.

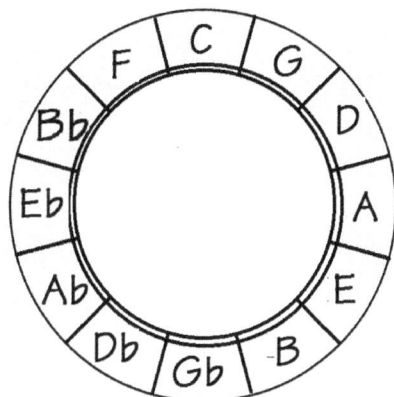

Clockwise, the wheel depicts a cycle of fifths. Counter-clockwise, it depicts a cycle of fourths, which is what you will be most concerned with.

If you could rotate the circle one chord position clockwise, the next chord in the cycle would come to the top. C resolves to F, which resolves to B♭ and so on.

But the circle is just a picture. It doesn't make sense until you hear it. And without multi-media, you can't hear a picture. One picture might be worth a thousand words in prose, but in music, two notes are worth a thousand pictures.

As you navigate the circle in a clockwise direction, each note, when looked at as the tonic note of its own major scale and the root note of its own chord, leads to the dominant note—the fifth—in that scale. Navigating counter-clockwise, each successive note is the subdominant note—the fourth—in the previous note's scale. Chapter 11 addresses their relationships in greater detail.

The Paths of Fifths/Fourths

Instead of a circle, which you cannot play, consider this path, which you can.

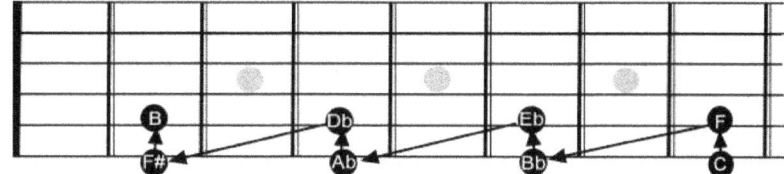

The illustration depicts the neck of your guitar as it appears to you when resting face up on your lap.

>   **Exercise:** Take the guitar off your lap and play the notes represented by the circles in the direction of the arrowed path.

The cycle isn't complete because it starts with C in this example and runs out of frets after B. But the pattern of the path is what you should notice.

>   **Exercise:** Slide the path up and down the fret board in either direction such that it starts on different notes, and the effects are the same; you're tracing the paths of chordal resolution.

Resolution

What does it mean when we say, for example, that C *resolves* to F? Those single notes in the path don't fully explain the concept of resolution. Each one is a tonic note to a chord, and the chords' other notes—thirds, fifths, and dominant sevenths—are what create the tensions that need to be resolved by the playing of a consequent chord and are what lured Chopin or Mozart from his deathbed to finish the resolution that someone else left unresolved.

The diagram just shown uses only strings 6 and 5 to describe the paths. But you can proceed another note up the strings and proceed through the path like this:

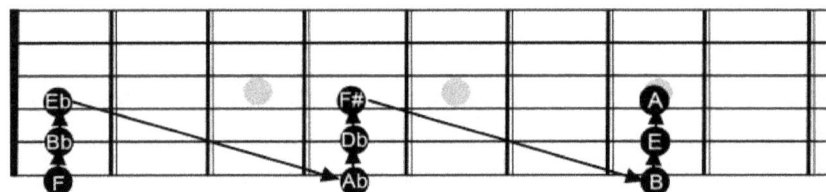

This path proceeds left to right because the frets to which you move to continue down the path are closer than they would be if you were going right to left as in the two-string path shown above. Nothing restricts you to either direction. It's shown here mainly for the convenience of the presentation.

As you might expect, you can use strings 6 through 3 the same way. We won't go that far, because the chordal system in these lessons uses strings 6 through 4 as the bottoms of the chords (the *root* notes explained earlier).

Those paths aren't the only ones that describe the circle of fifths. Those same notes can be found all over the fretboard. For example, the note F exists on the fretboard eleven times. The note C is on there twelve times. Do the math. 11 x 12 = 132 paths from C to F. You'll rarely use many of them, but they're there nonetheless. And that's only one interval. There are eleven more. The lucky guitarist has, therefore, over fifteen hundred ways to navigate from any given note to its fifth (or fourth, depending on which way you look at the wheel).

Chord Changes

So far all we've done is learn the single notes that are the roots of chords in the paths, and we've learned which notes lead to which next notes. But let's ask ourselves again how one chord can make the listener want to hear another specific chord. You'll need your guitar for this lesson. These are chords you've already seen in this book and probably elsewhere too.

The most important tones in a dominant 7 chord are the third and seventh.

Omit either of them and you remove the harmonic relevance of the chord to the rest of the passage that hosts the chord. Those notes are even more important than a chord's root and its fifth. A listener's brain will infer those tones if you leave them out. But leave out the third, and the listener can't distinguish between a dominant 7 and a minor 7. Leave out the seventh and there is nothing from which to resolve to the next chord.

Chapter 20 explains how the great rhythm jazz guitarist Freddie Green exploited these chordal characteristics.

Exercise: Play this C chord followed by this F chord and leave some silent space between. Maybe a couple seconds.

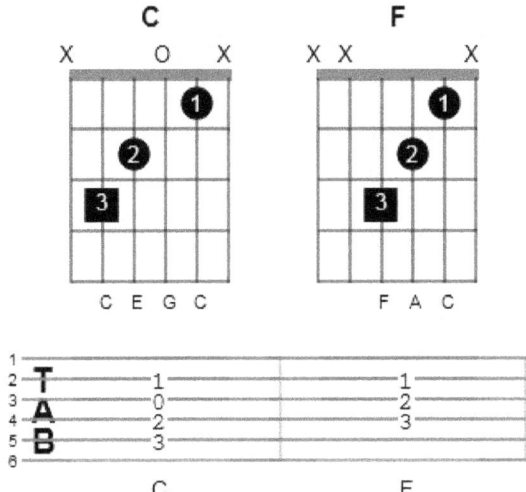

Not much about the C to F sequence creates any tension. You could quit after the C chord and nobody would care. Mozart and Chopin would stay in their beds. Nothing connects the two chords. The C could end a passage and the F could begin the next passage. At C, the ear says, "This is done. Move on." At F, the ear says, "We're at the start of another harmonic journey. Proceed."

It isn't always that way—little in music theory is always the same way—but as a general rule, it applies.

Exercise: Play the same two chords but add the dominant 7th note B♭ to the C chord.

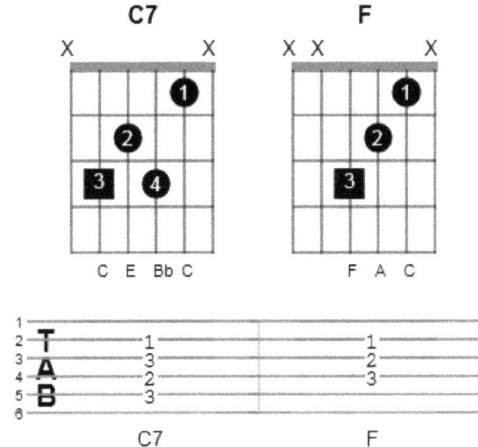

During the pause between chords, did you hear the tension? You can't walk away from that. It begs to be resolved. When you finally do play the F chord, the tension is resolved and the changes are complete. Nobody needs to come storming out of the bedroom to grab the guitar and hit that missing F chord.

The effect just demonstrated is harmonic resolution in a nutshell. The chords in a set of changes fit together because of one thing: they sound right within the context of the tune, which means they sound like what the listener expects to hear.

The resolution that the tension demands is found in the note you added to the C chord. That B♭—string 3, fret 3—demands to be resolved one half tone down to the F chord's A—string 3, fret 2, which is the F chord's 3rd.

Consequently, the resolution of C7 to F is not C to F as much as it is B♭ to A. If you leave those notes out of the changes, nothing has been resolved because no tension has been generated. Try it.

Exercise: Play these two chords in succession as you did above.

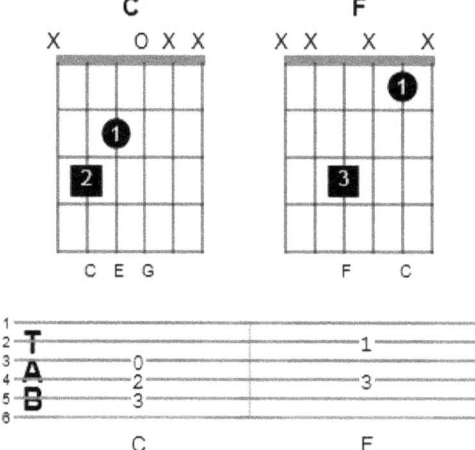

Hear the difference? With no dominant 7th (B♭) in the C chord, no tension is created. With no 3rd (A) in the F chord, there is nothing to resolve to.

Now don't jump to conclusions. All B♭s in chords in which B♭s occur do not demand to be resolved to chords that have an A. However, dominant 7th notes do wish to resolve to the 3rd of the next chord in the circle/cycle/path.

Chapter 9. Chord Colors

Chords are said to be either plain or embellished with what musicians call "colors," additional notes that don't really add to a chord's participation in the harmonic context but that make the chord sound fuller, "fatter," as they say, and more colorful. Another metaphor for these variations is "full-bodied" chords.

Chords with color are often easier to form than their so-called *vanilla* counterparts, and, since they are harmonically compatible, it's reason enough to use them. Another time to use them is when you are accompanying a *rubato* ballad, which means the tempo is variable as the tune progresses. A ballad with no beat. Chords with color sound fuller.

Playing rhythm swing accompaniment does not always need the colors. Vanilla chords work just fine particularly when the band includes bass and piano filling in the colors.

Vanilla Chords

Get your guitar out. To demonstrate the difference between vanilla and hip changes, we'll begin with the 1-6-2-5 changes Chapter 12) that you find in tunes such as *Blue Moon*, *Heart and Soul*, and many others. For now, it's enough to know that the numbers that identify these changes represent the chords based on the tonic, the sixth, the second, and the fifth chords.

Here are the vanilla 1-6-2-5 changes on a chord chart.

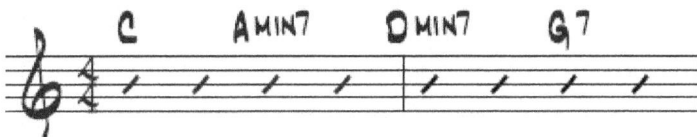

Here are the vanilla changes in grids.

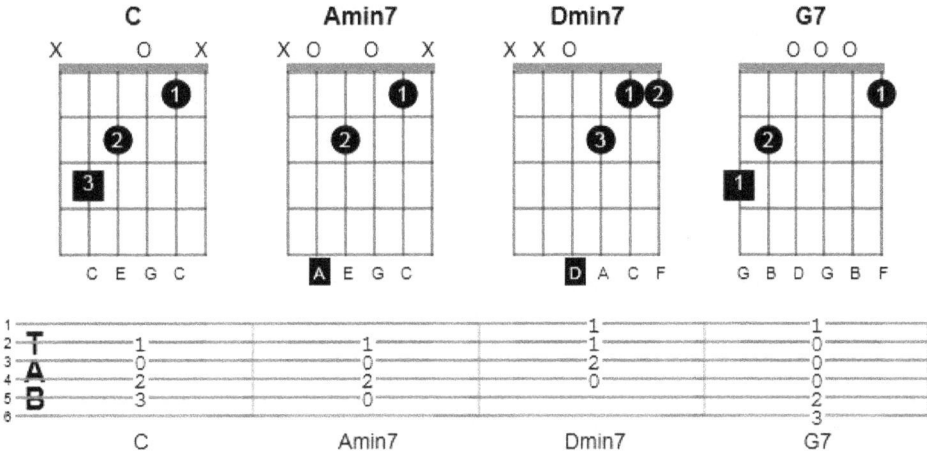

Note that each grid and tab gets two beats. Each pair of grids represents one measure on the chord chart. That's one of the confusing aspects of grid and tab notations: They don't specify rhythmic patterns—measures, time signatures, quarter notes, eighth notes, etc. They depend on your ear to do that.

   Exercise: Play these four chords repetitively to get a feeling for 1-6-2-5.

There's an important lesson to be learned from these two illustrations. The grids and tabs tell you what strings and frets to use for each chord. That's how you learn how the chords are formed. The chord chart above it tells you when to play each chord. That's how you will encounter guitar music in arrangements and fake books and on sheet music. When you know how to play all the chords by their symbols, the chord chart for a tune is all you need to play it.

If you have had much exposure to elementary guitar playing, you've probably seen all four of these chords. You'll learn more about them in Chapter 12.

> **Exercise:** Play the changes and hum along with *Blue Moon, Heart and Soul,* or any of countless pop tunes from bygone eras.

You might want to strum these chords rather than pluck them. All but the Dmin7 have more than four notes and the G7 has six.

The changes shown above, while they have potential, are, for lack of a better description, bland when played as solo accompaniment without other instruments contributing to the harmonies. The chords are vanilla, each chord containing only the tonic, 3rd and 5th, and, except for the opening chord, a dominant 7th. Guitar players have been using these chord forms since the guitar was invented.

Colorful Chords

Now consider these forms for the same changes.

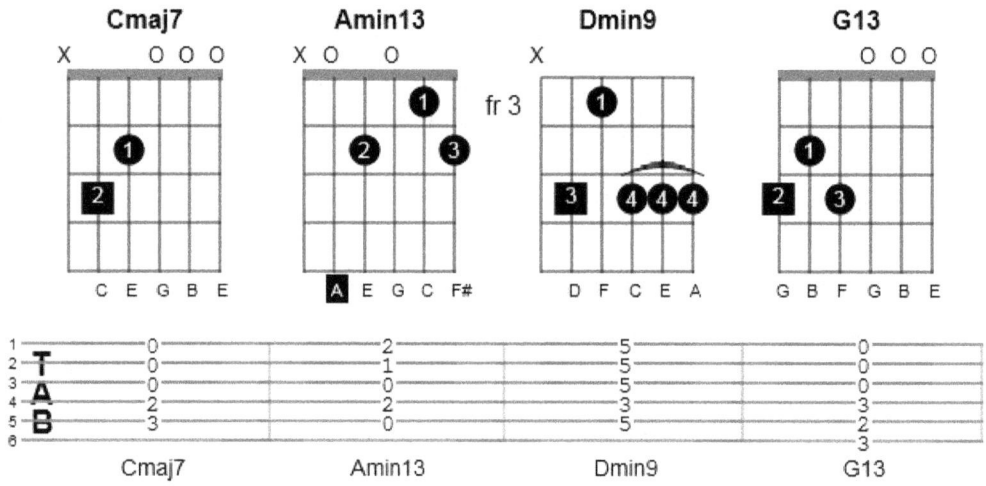

> **Exercise:** Using the same chord chart, strum this variation on 1-6-2-5 in C.

Observe the Cmaj7 chord. A major 7 chord is the major triad, C, E and G in this case, with the 7 added, which is B in this case. The string 2, which is note B, is open, forming a Cmaj7 chord. Sounds nice doesn't it?

When you play the 1-6-2-5 changes as they are formed in these grids and tabs, the vanilla 1-6-2-5 sound takes on substance. The chords are "fatter" and have more "color." This is the sound you want when you alone accompany vocals and solo instruments.

9 and 13

What, you might ask, are those numbers 9 and 13? You learned about the dominant 7th in Chapter 8. Now I'm tossing out 9s and 13s. What's with them?

Whenever you see a number greater than 7 in a chord symbol, if you don't know that specific chord, play the 7th. (Unless the chord is marked 69 or 6/9. See below.) A C7 works whenever the arrangement calls for a C9 or a C13. You won't be playing the full chord, but what you do play fits harmonically and doesn't create any dissonance.

The C7 works because the higher numbers imply the presence of a dominant 7th. A 9 chord has a dominant 7 and a 2 usually played above (at a higher pitch than) the 7th. 7 + 2 = 9. So C9 includes not only a B♭ (the dominant 7th) but a D (the second) as well. The C13 includes a sixth, which is an A. 7 + 6 = 13.

6, Maj7, and 6/9

Next we try three chord forms you can substitute wherever you see a major chord, in this example a C major. The 6 chord adds a 6th (A), the maj7 adds its major 7th. (B), and the 6/9 chord adds a 6th (A) and a 9th (D) above the root.

Those three chords aren't a set of changes. They're shown side by side for comparison. You don't have to practice them in sequence.

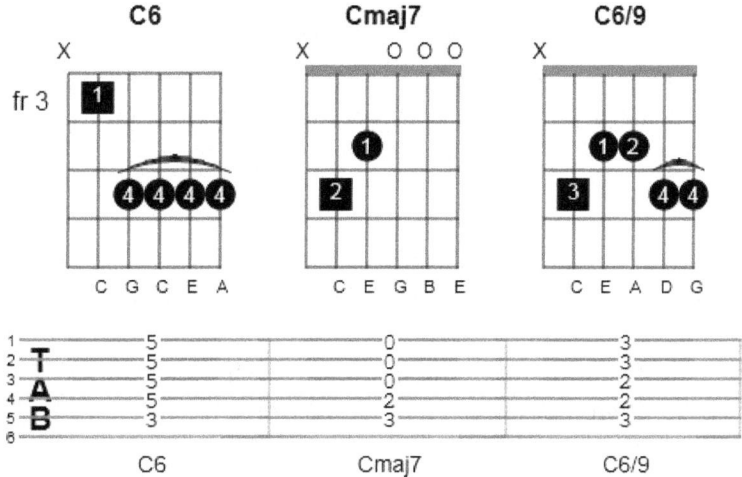

You can almost always use a 6 chord where a simple major chord is called for and that includes the 6/9 chord.

In some chord books the 6/9 chord does not include the 5th note, which in the grid above would mute string 1. In others it does. I've never encountered a situation where adding or removing the 5th has any effect on the harmonic context. That doesn't mean there's no reason for leaving the 5th out. It's just that I've never run into it.

The main thing to remember is that a 6/9 chord does not include the dominant 7 note, which in a C chord would be B♭.

You learn with experience when you can make these substitutions.

Whenever you see a simple major chord, you can usually play its major 7th. An exception is at the end of the tune when the singer is hanging on the key signature's root note, aka the *tonic*. Your B and the singer's C could clash.

You learned one form for the maj7 chord above. That form has open strings, but you can use the form with an index finger barre to move the form up the fretboard and play successive chromatic scale maj7 chords.

55

Here are three other forms for the Cmaj7 chord. These forms are transposable as well.

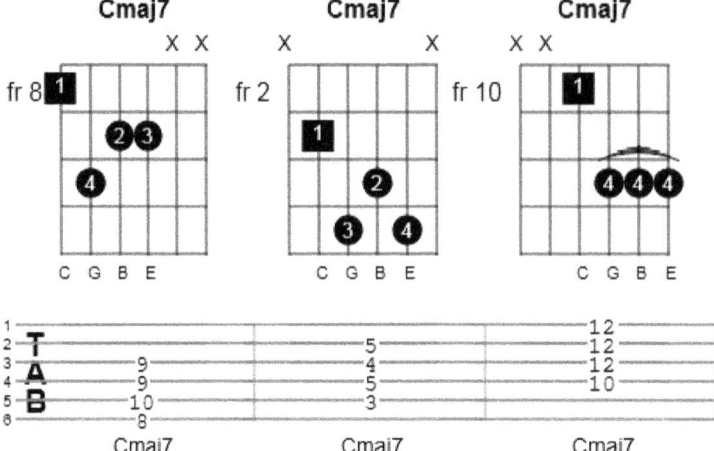

The distant hand positions demonstrate why you should know several forms for each chord. You usually want the form that is closest to where your left hand already is or where it's going next.

Vanilla vs Colors

Not all your chords need to be fattened. You have many vanilla chords at your disposal. Choose the chord that's most convenient to reach at the time and that you can easily play. When the band includes other chordal instruments, piano most often, you can play vanilla chords and let the pianist provide the colors. They're happier that way too.

You can also use vanilla chords to add a touch of grass roots to your sound. You'll learn when to be vanilla and when to be fat, and it won't always be the same chords at the same place.

There are other nice, fat, colorful, hip chord voicings, and we'll touch on some of them later, but for now, you've got a start on the road to prettier chords in your accompaniments.

Chapter 10. Tonal Centers

We know that a tune is usually written and played in a *key*. The key is usually the root of the concluding chord and the last note of the melody. Usually, but not always. Two tunes that end up in a different key than the one they start with are *Unforgettable* and *Why Did I Choose You*.

The *original* key is usually defined as the key in which the tune was originally published and is usually chosen so that the tonal range of the melody matches the vocal range of the typical male vocalist. Sorry, ladies, that's just how it's done. For purposes of this discussion, the original key is the one in which we are playing it, the one identified on charts by the key signature, or the one called out by whoever in the band calls the tunes and the keys.

The key of the composition or of an arrangement of the tune is expressed in its *key signature*, a number of sharps or flats encoded at the beginning of the standard notation. Guitar grids and tabs do not adhere to key signatures. They simply identify the notes to be played irrespective of the key signature.

A tune can, however, be written in more than one key. It can have phrases that modulate from the original key to a different one, usually returning to and ending with the original key later. (There are exceptions. Don't worry about them now.) These modulations change the tune's *tonal center*.

A tonal center, also called a *key center*, is the key in which a strain of a tune is played when it has modulated from the original key. Such modulations do not change the key signature. They just happen, and you play along with them fully expecting the tune to find its way back to the original key, the original tonal center.

An example is the bridge of the old tune, *Blue Moon* in the key of E♭ and shown here in a chord chart.

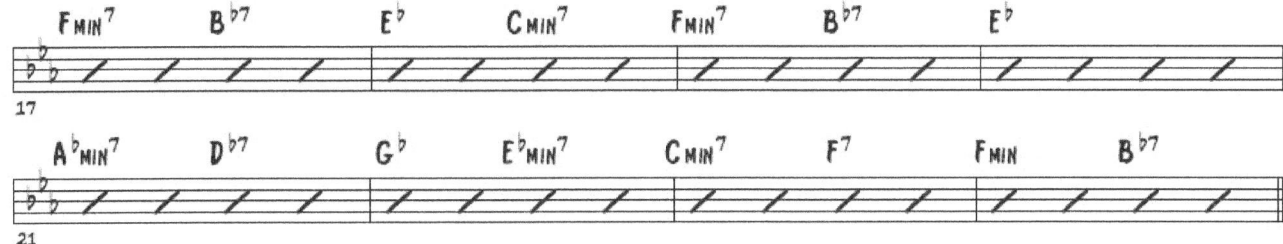

If you're unfamiliar with (too young for) *Blue Moon*, look it up on YouTube where you'll find several renditions. It was written in the 1930s by Richard Rogers and has had many renditions. Originally it was a ballad. Subsequently it made the charts with an up-tempo do-wop version and has been covered by Elvis, Sinatra, and every lounge singer since then.

> *Years back a local piano player was taking flying lessons. He almost had his license and he told the band's trumpet player that he'd like to take him for a ride after he got certified. The trumpet player pulled back and said, "You're nuts if you think I'm going up in a plane with a piano player who doesn't know the changes to the bridge to* Blue Moon.*"*

The bridge, which runs from measure 17 through measure 24, stays in tonal center C for the first four measures but with another common set of chord changes, in this case, Dmin7, G7, C, Amin7, the 2, 5, 1, 6 changes. The bridge then modulates to tonal center E♭ before returning to tonal center C.

That's two measures during which the tune is not in its original key. As complex as it might seem at first glance, this is a simple example, and you might wonder what the fuss is about. It illustrates harmonic behavior common to jazz and standard tunes. Some tunes stray much further from the original and move into multiple tonal centers before finding their way back to the original. The point is, you need to be aware of these changes, be able to recognize not only that the tonal center is changing, but what key it is in, and be able to play in that key.

The bridge to *Have you Met Miss Jones* changes tonal centers five times in eight measures, making it back to the original at the end of the bridge. Find a rendition of the tune on YouTube to hear what happens in the bridge, and follow along with this extract of the bridge. We are in the key of F in this example but the bridge begins in the B♭ tonal center.

The illustration shows the tonal centers for each melodic phrase above the measures. When the bridge begins, the refrain has ended with Cmin7, F7, which puts the bridge's first measure into the B♭ tonal center. The second measure of the bridge modulates into a G♭ tonal center which it stays in for one more measure. The fourth measure goes into D, the sixth measure into G♭ again, and the eighth measure returns to the original key of F.

There are many tunes in the jazz and standards repertoire that wander all over the tonal center map. Among them are *Joy Spring*, *All the Things You Are*, *Cherokee*, and *You Go to my Head*.

How do you identify a tonal center? Usually (but not always) the phrase in question resolves to the tonal center's major chord as happens with each of the tonal center changes shown for *Miss Jones*'s bridge. The three chords in each tonal center are called the ii-V-I changes, and the changes are so important to the playing of jazz (and many other kinds of music) that it has its own chapter in this book (Chapter 11).

Why do you care? Can't you just play the chords as written and not worry about an abstract theoretical detail such as the tonal center? Yes, you can if all you are doing is strumming along while a singer or instrumentalist carries the tune. But if you ever move into taking solos—and virtually every jazz guitar player does—the scales and tonal centers will suggest to you which improvised notes fit with each phrase of the tune.

PART IV. Changes

Part IV presents the *changes*, the sequences and progressions of chords you play that comprise a musical performance. Don't put your guitar away. The work has only just begun.

Chapter 11. Two-Five-One

The chord changes named "ii-V-I" and spoken "two-five-one" are the cornerstone of jazz harmonic construction as well as other music forms that depend on more than just the tonic-subdominant-dominant three-chord set. You saw it in the examples we've discussed in previous chapters. Complete books have been written about ii-V-I and virtually every book about playing jazz on any instrument includes a discussion that addresses ii-V-I.

Believe it or not, *much of your jazz playing involves playing simple ii-V-I changes*. Learn them and assimilate them into your playing, and you'll be comfortable with the majority of tunes you'll be called upon to play.

ii-V-I Major

The following changes are ii-V-I in the key of G. This is the vanilla version, the one you might have known before you began these lessons.

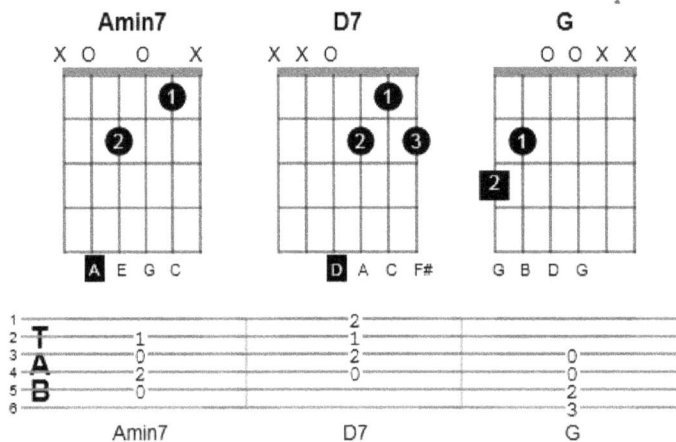

Exercise: Play these chords repetitively, two beats for the first two chords each and four beats for the third chord.

Here is ii-V-I in G fattened up some.

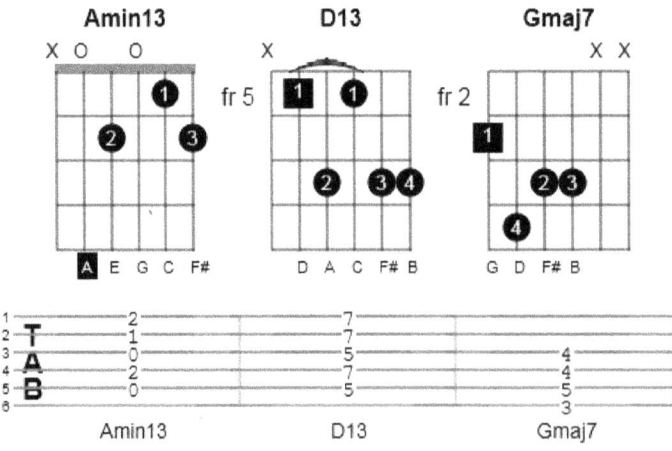

This combination of three forms sounds better but it has your hand jumping up and down the fretboard, and makes you think about where the root is for each chord. You jump from an open string 5 to fret 5, string 5 to fret 3, string 6.

Following are alternative changes of forms that make hand travel a bit easier.

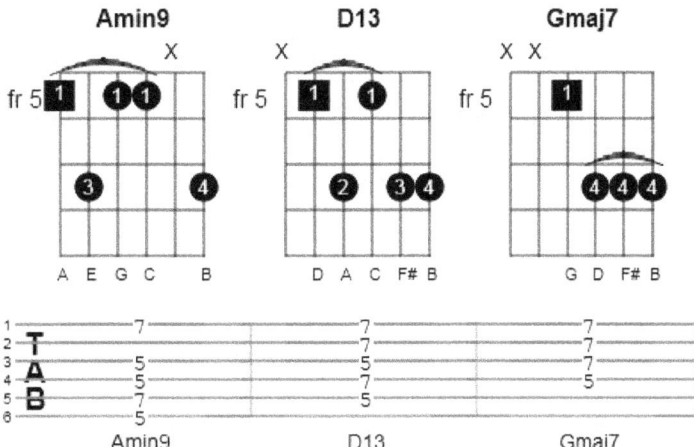

The roots for all three chords in the ii-V-I changes just shown are all on fret 5 and walk the path from string 6 to string 4. This combination of forms demonstrates how you can play some changes making the least hand movement up and down the fretboard for each chord and how you can choose the fret—5 in this case—because you know its note on string 6 of that fret—A in this case—and know intuitively that the two successive roots will be correct for the ii-V-I changed. How will you know that? You'll see later in this chapter.

Exercise: Play these changes repetitively as you did the vanilla version.

Here's a hint. Because of my small hands, I find the Amin9 and D13 chord forms difficult to play even though the left hand stays in the same position for all three chords. Here are alternative changes that are easier to play.

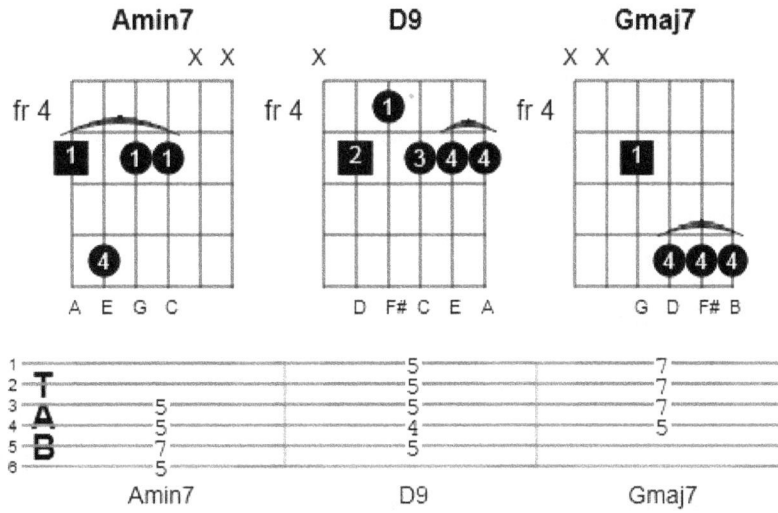

The root fret for all three chords remains the same, but my left hand moves down one fret for the second chord and back up for the third. (Follow where finger 1 goes to trace the hand movement.)

Exercise: Play these changes repetitively as you did the earlier two versions.

These forms for the ii-V-I changes are transposable, which means, as you learned in Chapter 6, you can move your left hand up and down the fretboard and get the same changes in different keys.

Exercise: Play these latest changes several times in each hand position beginning with fret 1 and proceeding chromatically up the finger board on each successive fret. Speak the names of the chord symbols as you progress. You don't need to speak the names of the fattened chords, just the vanilla ii-V-I names.

Here are the three-chord sequences starting in the first hand position and proceeding up the fretboard one fret at a time for four hand positions.

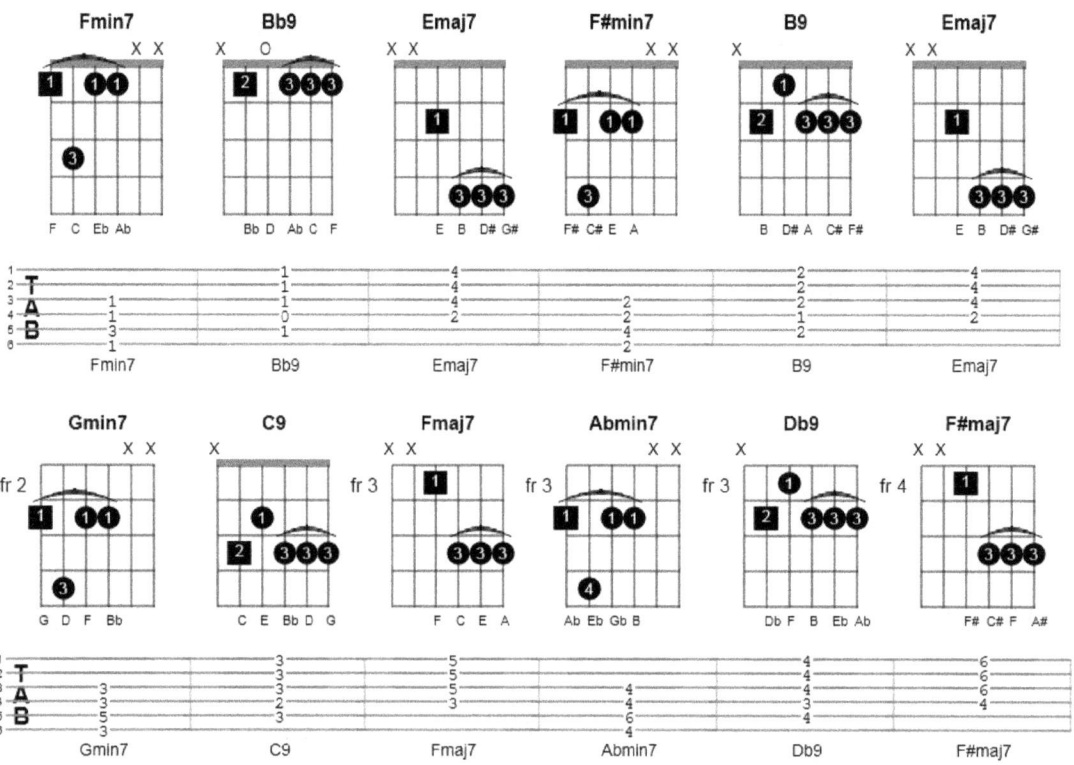

Note that the fret number varies to put the form close to the top of the grid except when the form fits on the grid with fret 1 at the top. This convention can vary depending on who's drawing the grid.

ii-V-I Basics

To understand ii-V-I, consider again the major scale. We'll use the key of C as an example.

C, D, E, F, G, A, B

Convert those letter note names to digits and you have the numbers associated with each note in the scale:

1, 2, 3, 4, 5, 6, 7

Add suffixes to form *ordinal numbers* and you have expressions to refer to the notes independent of which note is the tonic.

1st, 2nd, 3rd, 4th, 5th, 6th, 7th

...which, when spoken, are "first, second, third..." and so on.

Consequently, ii-V-I refers to the second, fifth, and first note in the scale. In the key of C, ii-V-I is D, G, C.

In this notation, lowercase Roman numerals designate a minor chord and uppercase designates a major chord. Again in C, ii-V-I becomes Dmin, G, C.

But wait. There's more. The ii and V shorthand notations represent dominant 7 chords. The I represents a major chord. Nothing in the shorthand tells you that; it's simply understood. So, given that ambiguity, the ii-V-I for the key of C is, finally:

Dmin7, G7, C

The following table illustrates ii-V-I for all twelve major keys.

Key	ii-V-I Changes
A	Bmin7, E7, A
Bb	Cmin7, F7, Bb
C	Dmin7, G7, C
Db	Ebmin7, Ab7, Db
D	Emin7, A7, D
Eb	Fmin7, Bb7, Eb
E	F#min7, B7, E
F	Gmin7, C7, F
Gb	Abmin7, Db7, Gb
G	Amin7, D7, G
Ab	Bbmin7, Eb7, Ab

Finding the Frets

Chord grids identify the fret number of the top/lowest/first fret on the grid. Unless you want to be counting frets almost every time you play a chord, you need a handy way to find the fret. The best way is to memorize which fret is which note on which string. That's a lot to remember—a guitar with twenty frets and six strings has 120 note positions—32 more notes than a piano—so it's best to start with string 6, which is closest to you, learn those notes, and remember the relative notes of adjacent strings.

If you know the note located at a given fret on string 6, you can be certain that strings 5 and 4 on the same fret are the next successive notes in the cycle of fourths. For example, if you know where A is on string 6, you'll know that string 5 is D and string 4 is G at that same fret.

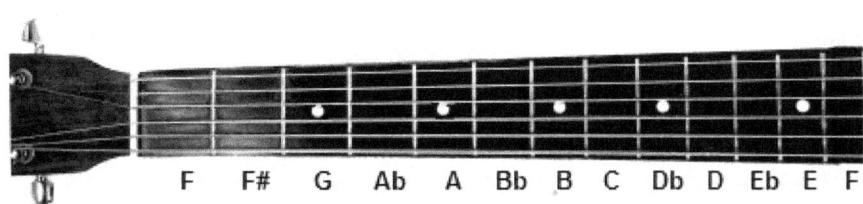

Take a look at your fretboard and compare it to this illustration, which shows string 6 notes for the first thirteen frets.

It shouldn't surprise you to learn that as you pluck your way up the fretboard on the same string, you are playing a chromatic scale. Each successive fret is a half-tone higher than the one that precedes it.

Chapter 4 explains the root notes on strings 4, 5, and 6.

Those dots on the fretboard are called *position markers* and are there to help you locate which fret you wish to play. Some guitars have ornate inlays instead of little dots, but their position and use are the same. They're like training wheels for the beginner. Experienced guitarists can sense where to position their left hand just from the feel of it, where the hand is, how the arm is bent at the elbow. Until you're at that point, use the position markers for reference.

Don't expect to play completely by feel and muscle memory, though. Watch the top jazz players on YouTube. They pretty much keep their eyes on the fretboard.

You're supposed to let the guitar hang flat against your belly when you play—which you have to do if you're standing up—and the position markers on the fretboard are out of sight. If you're sitting, tilting the guitar to where you can read the position markers can generate stress on your left wrist as you bend it to form chords. Not to worry, the top edge of the neck as it hangs from your strap has those little dots too. Just look down for the position marker you wish to use to orient your hand.

The illustration above provides the string 6 notes, but your guitar itself doesn't. A thin strip of painter's tape and a felt tip marker remedy that. Make sure you use the blue tape that doesn't leave residue when you pull it off. You won't need it for long. After a while, you'll have those notes fixed in your memory. Don't keep the tape on too long, however. You'll come to rely on it and it will not be there when you pick up another guitar.

Note that position markers are not much help if you use a capo. You have to orient your hand to the feel of the capo itself. Watch guitar players in videos who use capos. Their left hand usually stays close to the capo.

Walking the Paths

Here again is the fretboard illustration of the paths of fifths/fourths that you first saw in Chapter 8.

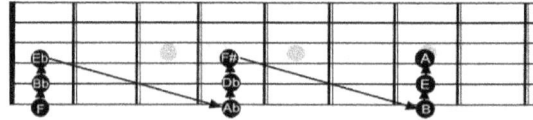

The three vertical notes in the path mirror the ii-V-I changes associated with the tonic, which in each vertical path is on string 4.

> **Exercise:** On fret 1, play a minor 7 form with the root at string 6, followed by a dominant 9 form with the root at string 5, and finishing with a maj7 chord with the root at string 4. Give each chord one strum and pause after the maj7 chord. Repeat the changes until you are comfortable with them. These changes are shown here as Fmin7, B♭9, E♭maj7.

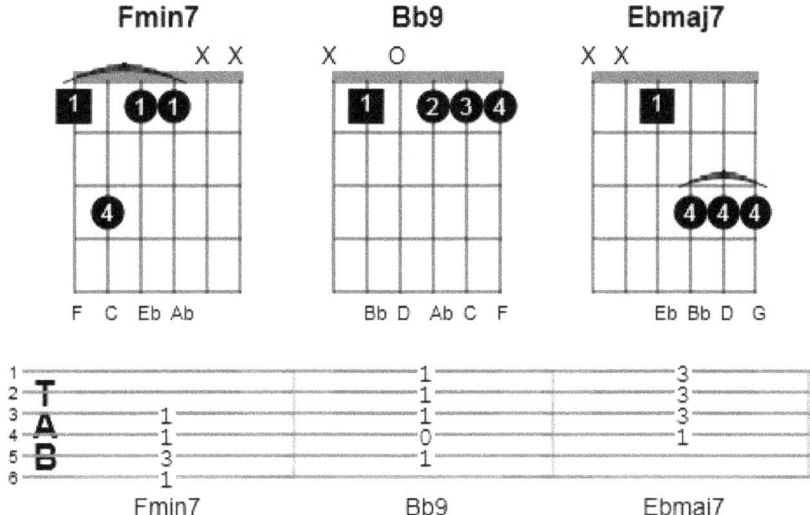

You have just played the basic ii-V-I changes with some fat tossed in for good measure. Observe that the root of each chord stays on fret 1 and moves from string 6 to string 5 to string 4 just as the fretboard illustration above shows.

Now let's add some structure to your practice.

Exercise: Begin with fret 2 and Play the changes once and say the name of each chord symbol in the changes out loud as you play the chord.

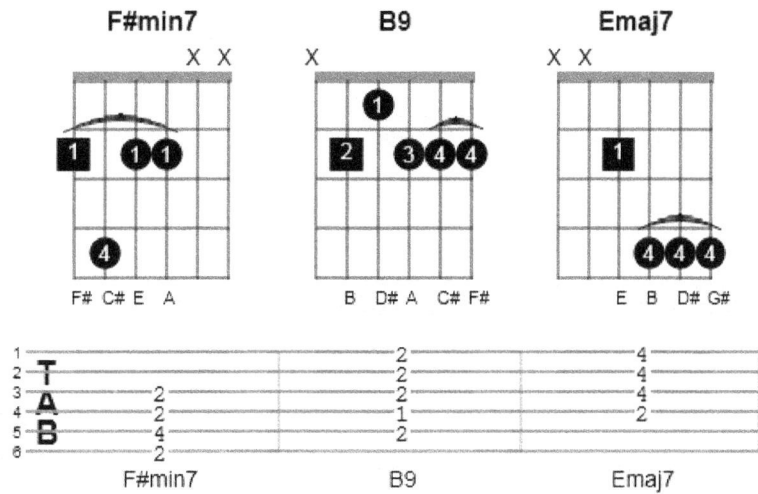

You have just played the ii-V-I changes in the tonal center of E. The chords are F#min7, B7, Emaj7, with of course, the colors added.

Exercise: Move your left hand one fret up and repeat the changes with the same forms. That's Gmin7, C9, Fmaj7. Again, say the chord symbol names out loud. Iterate this exercise for each fret. When you get to fret 12, reverse directions and repeat the exercise on the fret to the left. Continue until you're back at fret 1.

Repetitive ii-V

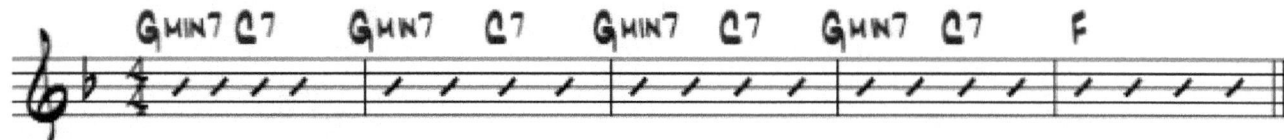

A common idiom in standard tunes is to repeat the ii-V changes multiple times before resolving to I. An example is *Honeysuckle Rose*, usually played in F. Here are the first five measures to illustrate the practice:

The tonal center for all five measures is F. The tune delays, however, the resolution and extends the tension by repeating the ii-V changes, Gmin7 to C7, three times before letting the third C7 resolve to the F.

Cherokee Bridge

The bridge to *Cherokee* demonstrates another ii-V-I variation.

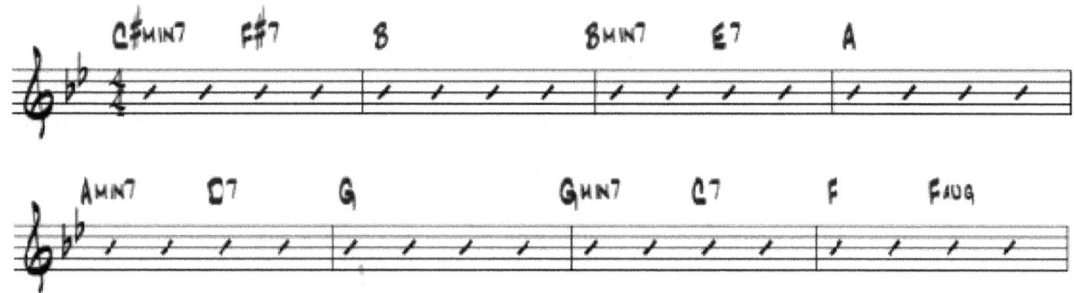

The tune is in B♭, but the bridge launches into the B tonal center without any modulation to resolve to it. It stays there for two measures and modulates into the A tonal center. This is interesting because the ii of A is Bmin7. The modulation happens when the tonic (B) of the previous tonal center is changed from a major chord to a minor 7 with the same root. B to Bmin7. The bridge repeats that pattern twice more, giving two measures to each tonal center. A to Amin7 and G to Gmin7. The tonal centers modulate down a whole step at a time: B to A to G to F.

Summary Chord Grids

To summarize, here are chord grids that demonstrate three forms with which you play the three chords that comprise the ii-V-I changes. I've used hand positions close to the nut. You can move your hand up the fretboard to make these chords with different roots. Each chord type (ii, V, or I) has three ways to form it depending on which string the root is on (6, 5, or 4). The chords shown here are vanilla forms and they are not presented as a progression. They are forms you can use in any hand position to make the chord based on the root of the form. There are no open strings in order to keep the chords transposable (Chapter 6).

Minor 7 (ii)

The following grids are not given here as a progression although you might play them in succession. They show three ways to form a minor 7 chord with the roots on strings 6, 5, and 4 respectively.

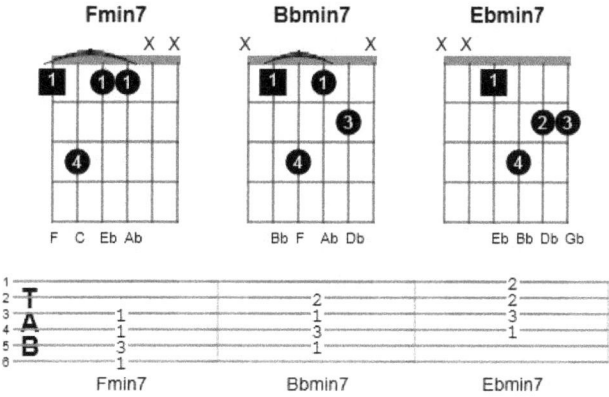

Exercise: As you practice these forms, move your left hand up the fretboard one fret at a time. You will then be playing F#min7, Bmin7, and Emin7, followed by a move to Gmin7, Cmin7, and Fmin7, and so on.

Dominant 7 (V)

The following grids are not given here as a progression although you might play them in succession. They show three ways to form a dominant 7 chord with the roots on strings 6, 5, and 4 respectively. Note that these are the vanilla forms for the chords.

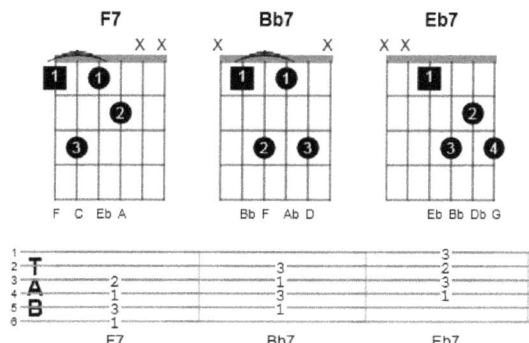

Exercise: As you practice these forms, move your left hand up the fretboard one fret at a time. You will then be playing F#7, B7, and E7, followed by a move to G7, C7, and F7, and so on.

Major (I)

The following grids are not given here as a progression although, here again, you might play them in succession. They show three ways to form a major chord with the roots on strings 6, 5, and 4 respectively.

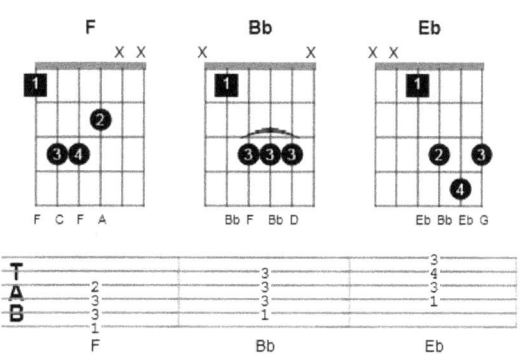

Exercise: As you practice these forms, move your left hand up the fretboard one fret at a time. You will then be playing F#, B, and E, followed by a move to G, C and F, and so on.

ii-V-i in Minor Keys

So far we've concentrated on ii-V-I as it applies to major key tonal centers. As you might expect, you can use the changes to resolve to a minor tonal center as well, which is spelled ii-V-i and pronounced the same as the major version, "two-five-one." The tune itself doesn't have to be in a minor key to use a ii-V-i, although it can.

First, let's look at a C minor scale.

C, D, E♭, F, G, A♭, B♭, C

C minor has three flats, the same flat notes as E♭ major, and they share a key signature. That's why C minor is called the *relative minor* key of E♭ and E♭ is the *relative* major of C.

Usually, but not always, the ii chord in these changes has its fifth flatted. If the tonal center is C, the ii chord is Dmin7(♭5) (Chapter 7), with the notes D, F, A♭, C. That is consistent with the key signature.

Often, but not always, the V chord in the ii-V-i changes is augmented (Chapter 7), which means its fifth is sharped. If the tonal center is C, the V chord is Gaug7, with the notes G, B, D#, F. D# is also E♭, so the Gaug7 is consistent too with the C minor key signature.

The third of the V chord keeps its original tone, which it needs to resolve to the i chord. This might seem inconsistent with the key signature, but it is consistent with, for example, the so-called *harmonic* minor key scale, in C minor for this example.

C, D, E♭, F, G, A♭, B, C

The following table illustrates ii-V-i for all twelve minor keys.

Key	ii-V-i changes
A minor	Bmin7(♭5), Eaug7, Amin
B♭ minor	Cmin7(♭5), Faug7, B♭min
C minor	Dmin7(♭5), Gaug7, Cmin
D♭ minor	E♭min7(♭5), A♭aug7, D♭min
D minor	Emin7(♭5), Aaug7, Dmin
E♭ minor	Fmin7(♭5), B♭aug7, E♭min
E minor	F#min7(♭5), Baug7, Emin
F minor	Gmin7(♭5), Caug7, Fmin
G♭ minor	A♭min7(♭5), D♭aug7, G♭min
G minor	Amin7(♭5), Daug7, Gmin
A♭ minor	B♭min7(♭5), E♭aug7, A♭min

Minor flat five and augmented chords are essential to jazz harmonies. Chapter 7 addressed them in detail. Here are the ii-V-i changes with transposable chords in tonal center C minor.

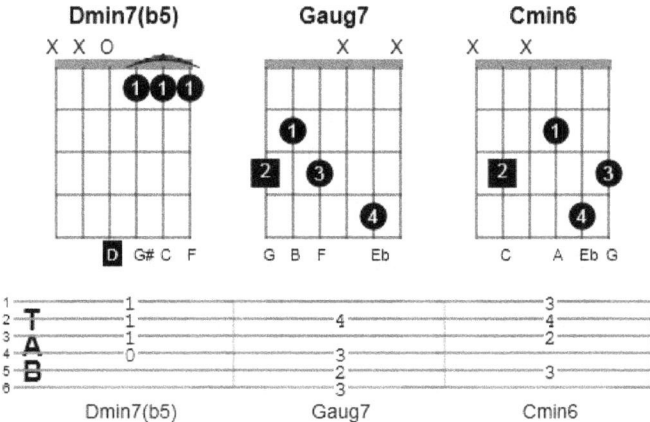

As often as not, the V chord is not augmented but only a dominant 7. It depends on the melody, the harmonic context, and the band's interpretation. Keep an eye and ear on the changes that have been written down or agreed to.

Here are more ii-V-i changes but in B♭ minor with the first root on string 5.

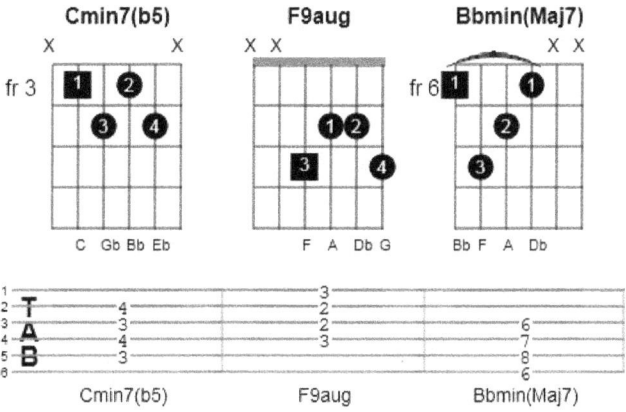

And here it is in E♭ minor and starting on string 6.

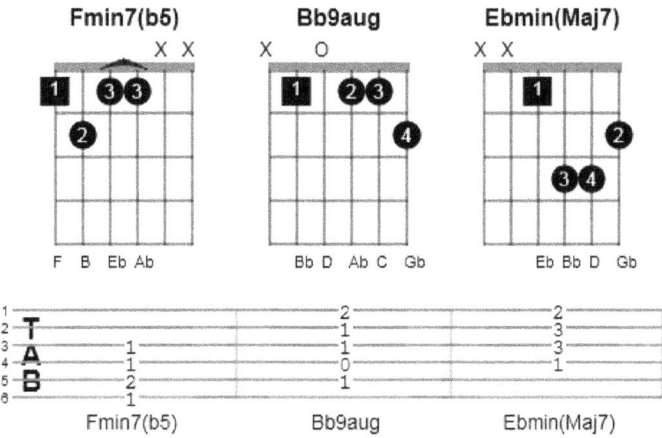

The B♭9 form is not transposable up and down the fretboard. The other two are. You could make it transposable by muting string 4, which would mute the chord's 3rd note (D).

Chapter 12. One-Six-Two-Five

If ii-V-I (Chapter 11) are the cornerstone of jazz harmonies, 1-6-2-5 are the foundation. Countless old tunes use the 1-6-2-5 changes for their refrains, among them, *Blue Moon, Heart and Soul, The Devil and the Deep Blue Sea, I Got Rhythm* (Chapter 14), and many more.

> *Blue Moon is one of two tunes that kids learn to play in duo on the piano. The other one is* Heart and Soul. *One kid plays the bass, note, chord, note, chord in the key of C. The other kid plays the melody. My cousin and I almost drove my aunt to drink with those renditions when we were kids.*

The only changes more common are the Blues (Chapter 13). The 1-6-2-5 changes are so common in jazz and standards that you will come to recognize them as soon as you see them on a chart.

Chapter 9 introduced 1-6-2-5 as a way to illustrate adding colors to chords. Now, we'll look at them in more detail. Here are the colorful changes in the key of F with transposable forms (Chapter 6).

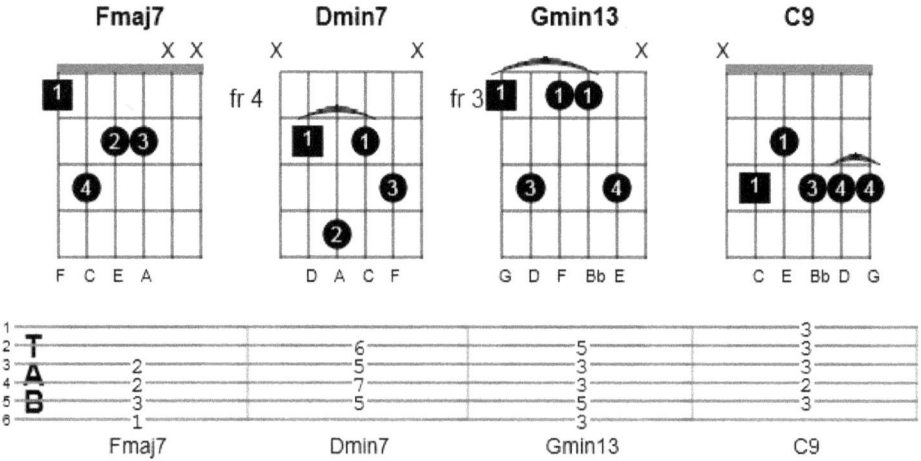

And here are the vanilla changes as you might see them on a chart.

Often you'll substitute a dominant 7 chord for the minor 7 chord in the first measure. That would make these changes: F, D7, Gmin7, C7.

> **Exercise:** Practice the 1-6-2-5 changes repetitively. It might seem like you are playing a vamp, which is a repetitive intro (Chapter 15) to or interlude within a tune awaiting a go-ahead signal from the leader.

> **Exercise:** Practice the 1-6-2-5 changes for each left hand position, moving your hand up the fretboard one fret position at a time for each playing to change the tonal center. Speak the names of the chords as you change positions.

There's not much more to 1-6-2-5 than that. You'll use the changes many times in your playing, in the refrains of some tunes, in the bridges (Chapter 15) of others. You'll use them for introductions, turnarounds (Chapter 15), and interludes whenever someone wants to talk to the audience while there's music playing in the background.

teach yourself Rhythm Jazz Guitar, *a player's guide* – Al Stevens

The following table illustrates 1-6-2-5 for all twelve major keys.

Key	1-6-2-5 Changes
A	A, F#, Bmin7, E7
B♭	B♭, Gmin7, Cmin7, F7
C	C, Amin7, Dmin7, G7
D♭	D♭, B♭min7, E♭min7, A♭7
D	D, Bmin7, Emin7, A7
E♭	E♭, Cmin7, Fmin7, B♭7
E	E, C#min7, F#min7, B7
F	F, Dmin7, Gmin7, C7
G♭	G♭, E♭min7, A♭min7, D♭7
G	G, Emin7, Amin7, D7
A♭	A♭, Fmin7, B♭min7, E♭7

Of course, these are the vanilla changes. You'll want to color them wherever possible.

Chapter 13. The Blues

The 12-bar *blues* are among the most commonly used chord changes in traditional jazz. It is also a staple of country-western and old time rock 'n' roll. There are several variations to the blues, usually depending on the kind of blues being played.

Blues has its foundations in field and gospel songs from the South toward the end of the nineteenth century. Composer W.C. Handy immortalized blues changes by bringing them into mainstream popular music. His tunes *St. Louis Blues*, *Memphis Blues*, and others used the basic blues changes and set the standard that's been followed for more than a century.

Major Blues

Here is the traditional twelve-bar major blues chord changes in the key of G. We'll begin with a chord chart so you can become accustomed to the format you'll read on gigs.

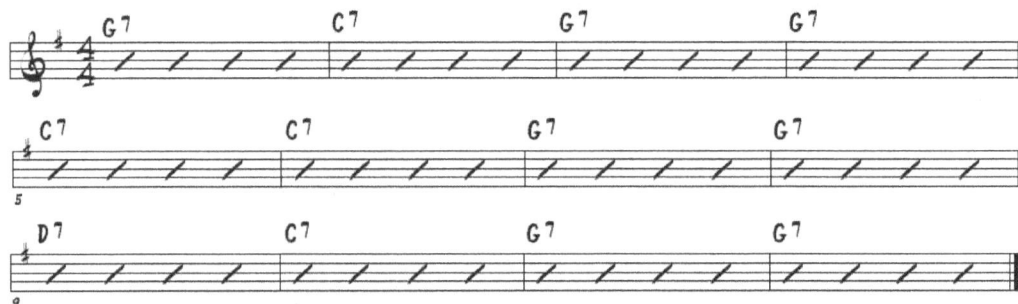

In some 12-bar blues versions, particularly in the old time rock 'n' roll genre, the second measure remains on the tonic chord, which is G7 in this example. The first rock tune I recall hearing, *Rock Around the Clock*, stays with the tonic.

Here are the grids and tablature for *Blues in G*. Although the chord chart calls for vanilla chords, we've fattened them up in the spirit of these lessons. Each grid in these changes represents one measure in the chord chart and gets four beats.

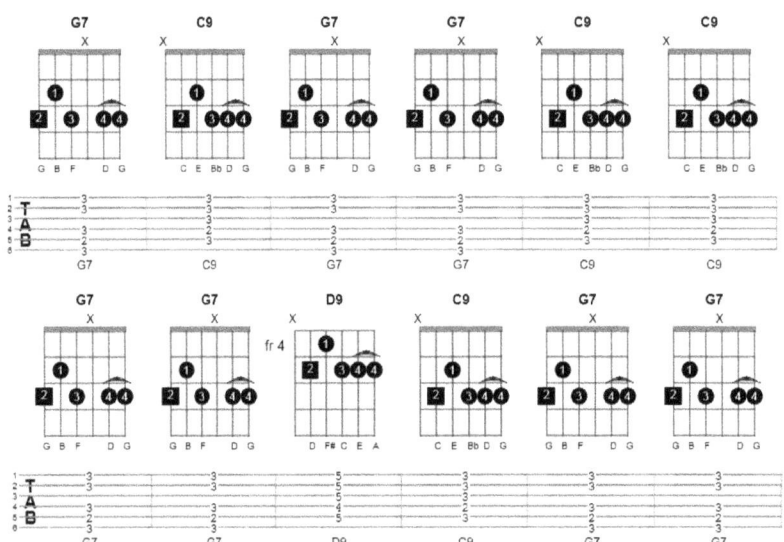

72

Exercise: Play *Blues in G* from the grids and tablature until you have it memorized. Then refer back to the chord chart and play the changes while you read the chart. The idea is to impress into your brain and muscle memories the associations between the chord symbols and their forms and positions.

Exercise: With the blues under your belt, practice the changes at various tempos from slow, down and dirty (approx. 70 beats per minute) to a top speed swing tempo (approx. 200 bpm). Don't worry if the faster tempo doesn't come to you right away. Get it going as fast as you can and then set it aside for a while.

Exercise: To understand how transportable these chord forms are (Chapter 6) use the same grids and play the blues in the key of B♭. To do this, move your hand up three positions.

The grids will look exactly like the ones above for blues in G, but the fret numbers will be higher and the chords will be:

B♭7, E♭9, B♭7, B♭7, E♭9, E♭9, B♭7, B♭7, F7, E♭9, B♭7, B♭7

Exercise: Using the same forms, play the blues in the key of F. To do this, you'll move your hand to the first position with string 5 open except for the C9 chord. To do this, just raise your index finger or finger the forms differently like this (each chord shown only once):

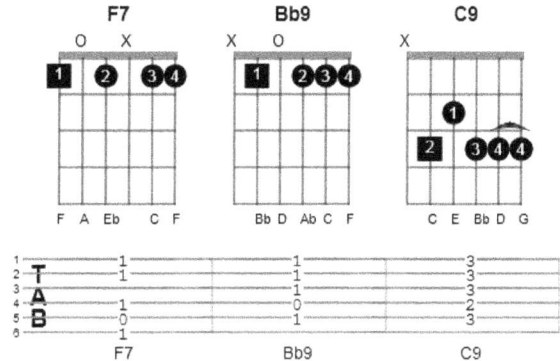

The F7 and 9 are examples of open string transposable chord forms. Notice that C9 is the same form you used for the same chord when you played the blues in G.

However, as you would expect, B♭9 is a different form from the B♭7 you used with blues in B♭. Here are the two forms:

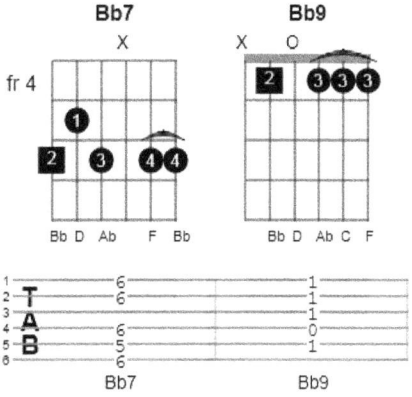

Recall from Chapter 9 that you can use a 9th wherever you see a 7th and vice versa. The two chords are interchangeable within the harmonic context of the tonal center. Play them side by side to hear the common harmonic sound and the coloring difference that adding the 9 (C) gives to the sound.

The most frequently played blues are in F, B♭, and G in that order of precedence, so those are the ones you should be most familiar with. Jazz players love the key of F, calling it the *mother key*.

The 12-bar blues changes have many variations. You'll learn about some of them in Chapter 16.

Minor Blues

You can play the twelve-bar blues in minor keys too. Here are the changes in G minor.

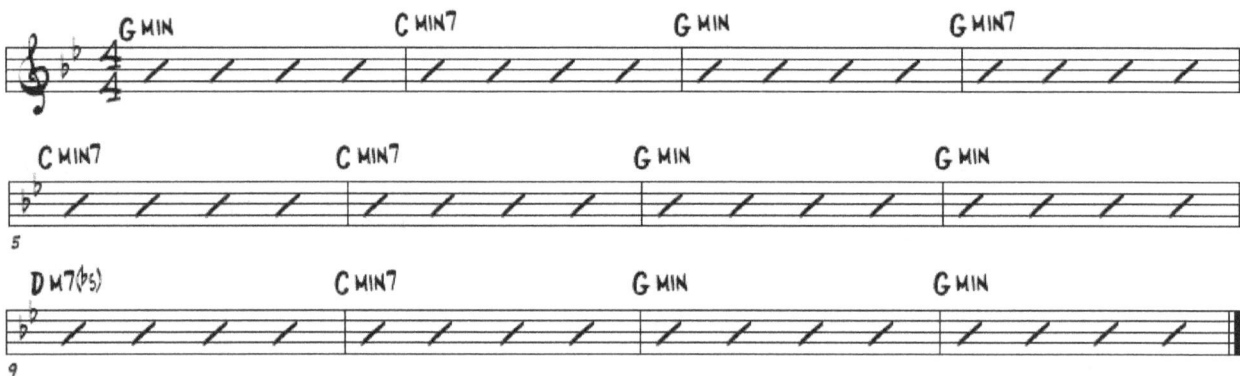

All the notes in all the chords in a minor blues are members of the minor key's scale.

Non-blues Blues

Many tunes are titled *blues* that do not use the 12-bar blues changes. Many others use them for one refrain and other changes for others. Examples are: *Beale Street Blues*, *Blues in the Night*, and *Tishomingo Blues*. *St. Louis Blues*, uses the usual 12-bar blues changes for two of its three refrains and a 16-bar minor key refrain for the other.

Chapter 14. Rhythm Changes

You learned the 1-6-2-5 changes in Chapter 12.

This chart contains *Rhythm Changes*, the jazz musician's name for the changes to *I Got Rhythm*, which happen to be the changes to many other tunes.

Be-boppers adapted the changes to *I Got Rhythm* in so many of their jazz tunes that the changes are identified as simply "Rhythm changes," which they applied to such tunes as *Oleo*, *Cottontail*, and countless others. These changes were used for the theme song to the TV cartoon series, *The Flintstones*.

These are the vanilla changes. You can substitute the colorful ones.

These changes are to an AABA tune, which is musician's shorthand for a tune that has two eight-measure refrains, which are called the A parts, followed by an eight-measure bridge called the B part, and ending with another eight-measure A part. Many tunes that you'll play will either follow that format or come close.

More contemporary jazz tunes can go off on harmonic and structural tangents, and more recent pop music styles such as punk, heavy metal, hip-hop, and others, don't seem to follow any patterns at all. Not a criticism, just how they are.

AABA seems to be a "tin pan alley" innovation. Earlier tunes from the Great American Songbook favor a format with two 16-measure passages.

The tune *After You've Gone*, which we discussed in Chapter 5, is an example of a tune that is not in AABA format. There are many others.

Rhythm's refrain version of 1,6,2,5 uses a dominant 7 rather than a minor 7 for the 6 chord. This is a common substitution. Here are the fattened 1,6,2,5 changes in Bb:

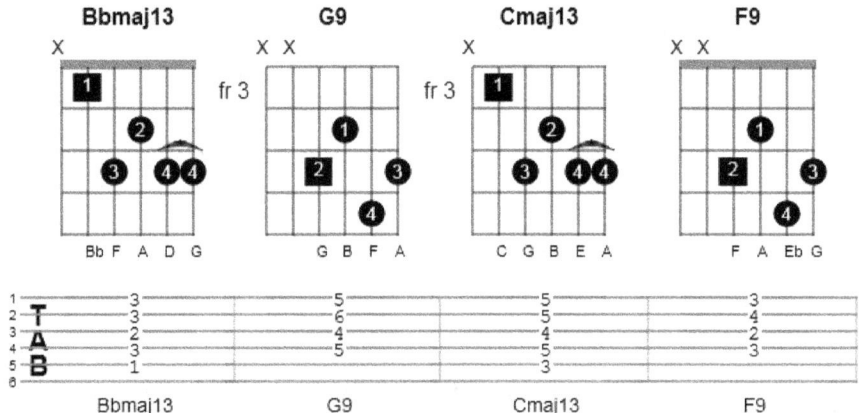

The two pairs of chords have the same forms but on different frets. This is a good exercise for walking the 1,6,2,5 path, going from string 5 to string 4 with the roots and moving up two frets at a time.

Rhythm substitutes a 3-minor 7 chord for the first chord of the second four measures, making it 3,6,2,5 changes, frequently used for refrains, bridges, and turnarounds (Chapter 15).

Rhythm Bridge

The bridge to Rhythm changes—measures 17 through 24—is also 3,6,2,5. The chords in the bridge are all dominant 7s and they walk the path of fourths to get back to the tonic chord in the last eight measures. Here are those changes fattened up.

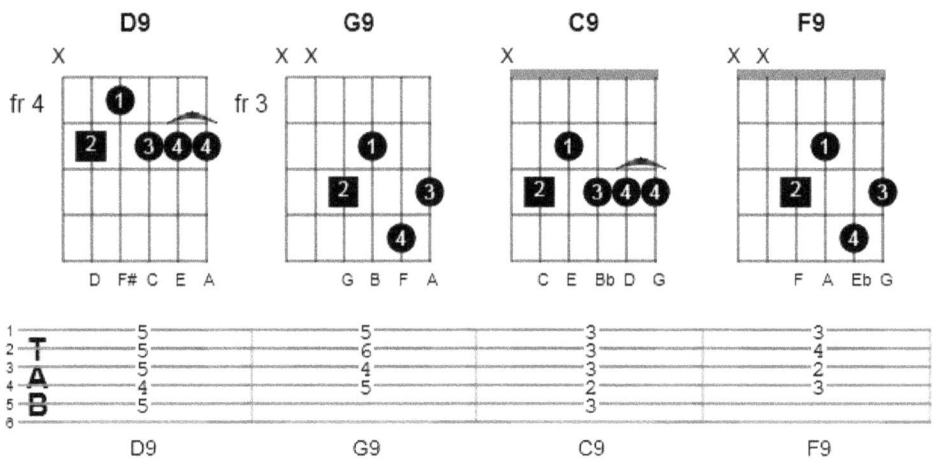

These chords get eight beats—two measures—each. Observe that the two pairs share forms as in the 1,6,2,5 above, but this time they follow the path of fourths. Another good exercise for your practice sessions.

These changes are commonly called the "Sears Roebuck bridge" among musicians (Chapter 15).

A common substitution precedes each dominant 7 chord with the minor 7 that would resolve to it, its own subdominant. Chapter 16 goes into more detail about this substitution.

Tag

The original tune, *I Got Rhythm*, on which these changes are based, includes a *tag* at the end (Chapter 15). The chord chart above doesn't have that tag because most adaptations of Rhythm changes in other tunes do not include a tag at the end but play the tune as a usual 32-measure AABA tune (Chapter 15) and maybe a tag at the end but not always. We'll talk more about tags in Chapter 15.

Chapter 15. Passages

Jazz and standard tunes often follow familiar patterns that musicians are accustomed to playing. These patterns employ *passages* of different kinds to comprise the tune.

The Chorus

The *chorus* is the outer passage, the main part of the tune, beginning to end, the part everyone is familiar with. The chorus contains and is surrounded by other passages.

The following chord chart for the very old tune, *Ain't She Sweet*, is the chorus of that tune, and it follows the AABA format.

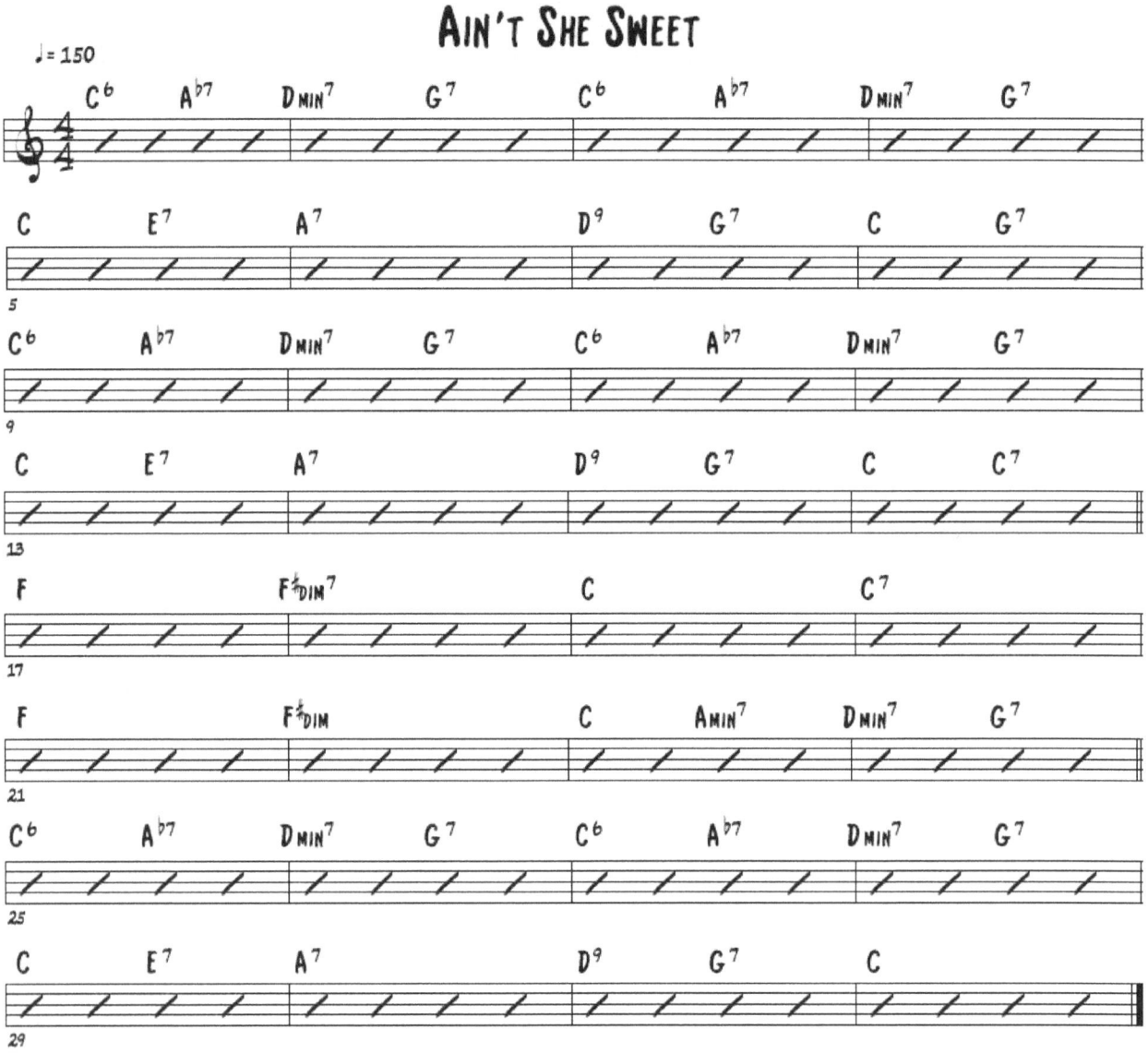

Any tune can contain other identifiable passages, such as intros, turnarounds, tags, and endings. We'll explore these harmonic passages. If you see a chord you haven't learned, refer to Appendix A to view the various ways you can form it.

Intros

Jazz tunes often begin with an *intro* or "introduction," a musical passage that gets the tune started and sets up the first tonal center, which is usually the tune's key signature. It tells the musicians and singers when to come in. If you're reading from an arrangement, the intro is written for you and you just read it like you do the rest of the chart. If you're playing in a jam session or at a gig where you're playing a so-called *head* tune, one that everyone knows well enough to play by ear, the rhythm section plays the intro, and the leader tells the band how the intro goes by saying one of these:

"Start on top." This means there is to be no intro and the band begins playing the tune at its opening passage. Sometimes in a noisy room the leader uses sign language by tapping the top of his head with his palm. That also means "go back to the top" when you're improvising choruses.

"Four bars," or "eight bars." This tells the rhythm section to improvise an intro of four or eight bars, one that naturally segues into the tune's first refrain.

"Last four," or "last eight." The rhythm section is to play the last four or eight bars of the tune, which naturally segues into the top.

"Bring us in." If the tune is a ballad and there is a singer, the leader is telling the piano or guitar player to play a solo intro in a *rubato* tempo, which is free-style. The singer will come in where appropriate (you hope) and the leader will count the band in when the tempo is supposed to become a regular beat.

There are many changes for improvised intros, some well known, others left to the player's fancy. Here is a generic intro in the key of C that can lead the chorus or verse into any tune that begins with a C chord.

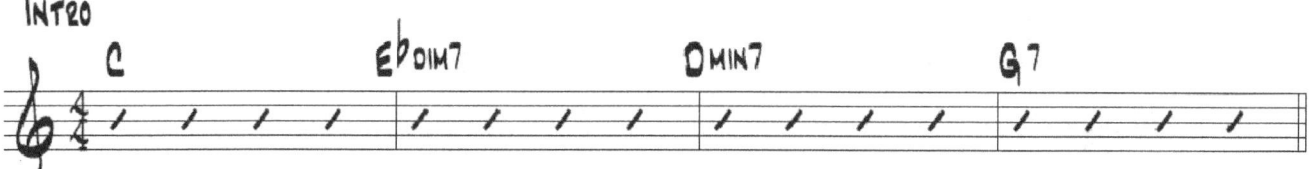

Sometimes the leader asks for an eight-bar intro. Players often use the last eight bars of the chorus as the intro. Here is such an intro that can be used with many standard tunes that begin with the IV chord.

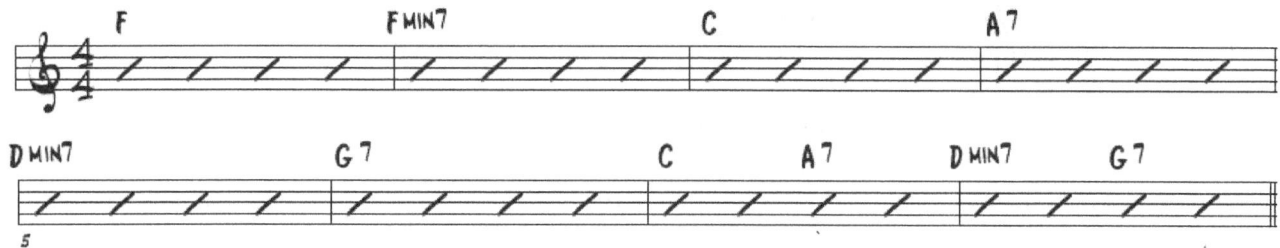

After playing six of the tune's last eight measures, the player inserts a 1-6-2-5 (Chapter 12) turnaround passage to bring in the top of the chorus.

This intro is generic. It fits many tunes.

If the band includes a piano player, it's best for the guitar player to sit out the intro and leave it to the piano player. This avoids harmonic clashes. If the leader wants a guitar intro, then the piano player usually sits out the intro.

The only rule—guideline, actually—for intros is that they end in a chord that resolves to the first chord of the tune's beginning refrain. If the tune is in C and starts on a C chord, the intro should end on a G7 chord. If the tune is in C and starts on an F chord—*After You've Gone*, for example—the intro should end on a C7 chord to resolve to the F in the first measure of the chorus.

Verses

Many tunes, particularly standards and show tunes, have a *verse*, which is a musical preface to the tune's chorus. Bands leave the verse out—not everyone knows the verse. To play or not to play the verse is a bandstand call. Sometimes I like verses more than the chorus itself. Vocalists like to sing verses because the lyrics, particularly in ballads, can be haunting as they offer a promise of a story to be told.

A nice verse can lead to a surprise for the audience because they're unfamiliar with it. You begin playing or singing the verse, often in rubato, and they don't know what tune is coming. When you reach the first chorus and they hear its familiar refrain, their tension is relaxed and they often break into applause.

Over the Rainbow has a beautiful verse that Judy Garland did not sing in the *Wizard of Oz* movie. When you play it, the audience is on the edge of their seats waiting to hear what's next. When they hear the first two notes, "Some-where..." they find out.

The verse that virtually everyone is familiar with is the verse to Hoagy Carmichael's *Stardust*. It's familiar because virtually every rendition of *Stardust* includes the verse, which is usually sung or played *rubato*, leading to the chorus in tempo.

> *Frank Sinatra recorded a version of Stardust in which the verse was the complete tune. He did not record the chorus. His explanation was that the Stardust verse is a beautiful song on its own. Legend has it that Carmichael was at first disturbed by Sinatra's omission of the chorus but changed his mind when he heard the recording.*

Turnarounds

A *turnaround* is a passage with which a player transitions between parts of the tune. Turnarounds usually and typically get you from the first A part to the second A part and from the third A part back to the top of the chorus. A turnaround is typically 1,6,2,5 if the next passage stays in the original tonal center and begins with that tonal center's tonic chord. Otherwise the turnaround uses a dominant 7 chord to resolve to the first chord of the next passage.

The last two measures of the intro shown a few paragraphs back is a typical 1-6-2-5 (Chapter 12) turnaround.

Bridge

The *bridge*, also called the *release*, is part B in an AABA tune. The bridge usually has different changes and melody from the A parts. Some tunes don't have bridges.

> *A tourist gets lost in Louisville, Kentucky. He pulls over and hails a musician walking down the street.*
>
> *"Pardon me, sir," the tourist asks. "Where is the bridge to Indiana?"*
>
> *The musician replies, "There ain't no bridge to Indiana," and goes on his way.*

If you hum *Take me Back to Indiana* or any of the be-bop tunes that are derived from the *Indiana* changes—*Donna Lee*, for example—you'll find that it consists of two sixteen-bar refrains and does not follow AABA at all. *Sweet Georgia Brown* goes without a bridge too as does its derivative jazz standard, *Dig*. The Less Paul, Mary Ford classic, *How High the Moon*, which donated its changes to Charlie Parker's *Ornithology*, has no bridge. And, *After You've Gone*, which we used to demonstrate Nashville, Numeric, and Internet notation (Chapter 5) has no bridge.

Generic IV Bridge

Many pop, country, rock, and folk AABA songs use these generic bridge changes. You'll play it so many times you can play it in your sleep. It begins on a IV chord and proceeds for 8 measures to return to the C chord that begins the third A part.

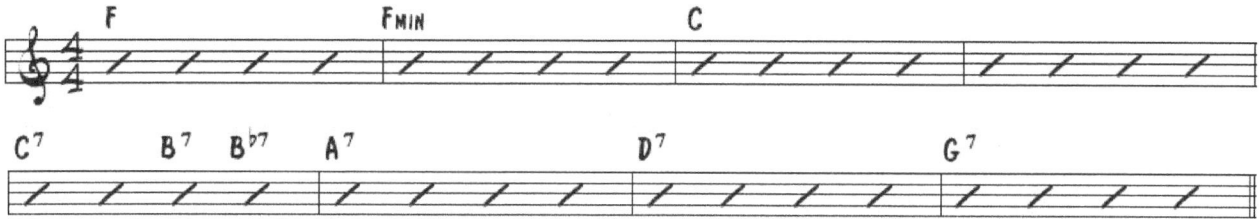

Here's a variation, also found in many tunes.

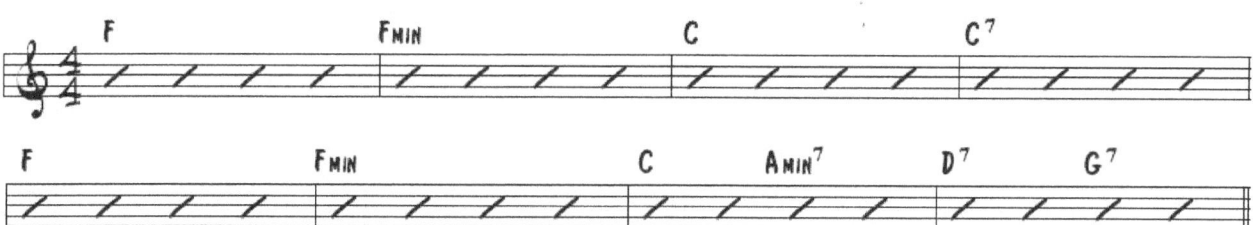

Some tunes use the F#dim7 in the second measure of these bridges.

There are other generic bridge chord changes. You'll run into a lot of them as your playing experience expands.

Sears Roebuck Bridge

The *Sears Roebuck* bridge is an eight-bar chord sequence that many tunes use for their bridges, changing only the melody. The bridge is the same one you learned for the Rhythm changes in Chapter 14. It uses a four chord progression with each chord getting eight beats or two measures. Here's that bridge again.

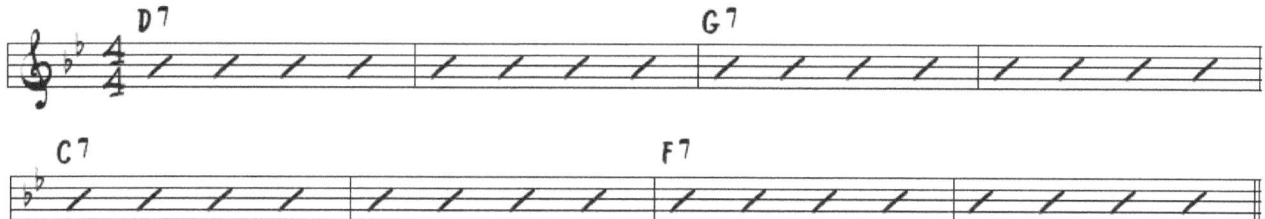

It is not unusual for musicians to expand these changes to make them more interesting. They might, for example, precede each of the dominant 7 chords with the minor 7 chord that resolves to it (Chapter 16).

Depending on your age, you might recognize the Sears Roebuck bridge from the old tune, *Five Foot Two*. The be-bop standards, *Cottontail*, *Oleo*, *Scrapple from the Apple*, *Perdido*, and many others use these changes in their bridges.

Montgomery Ward Bridge

The *Montgomery Ward* bridge is almost a cliché in old standards. Examples are *On the Sunny Side of the Street*, *Satin Doll*, and *Honeysuckle Rose*, and countless others. You'll find it in jazz tunes as well.

Montgomery Ward begins with the key signature's tonic chord in dominant 7 form. If you are playing in C, the first chord of the bridge is C7 as shown here.

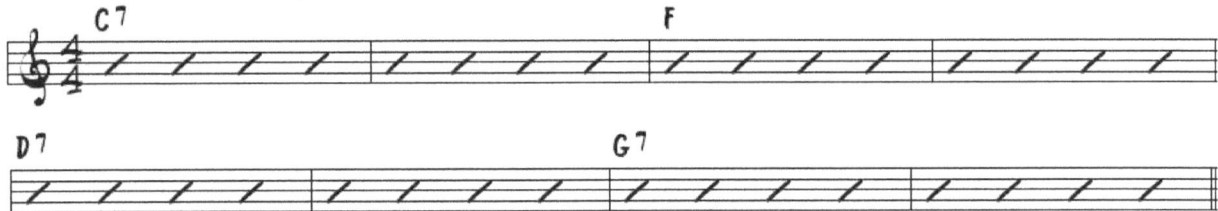

Each chord lasts two measures and then resolves to the next chord in the circle of fifths. This pattern ends with the dominant 7 of the key signature's dominant chord (the 5th), G7 in this case, which resolves to the key signature's tonic chord to begin the third A part of the AABA format.

The bridge to *Honeysuckle Rose* teaches other lessons. It's a variation of Montgomery Ward that doesn't stay on the dominant 7 chords that walk it through the cycle. Instead, it uses passing chords that ascend from the current dominant 7 to the next one. In the key of F, the original, the bridge starts on the tonic dominant 7, F7. Instead of hanging there for two measures, it walks F to G to A♭ to A on its way to the B♭ resolution.

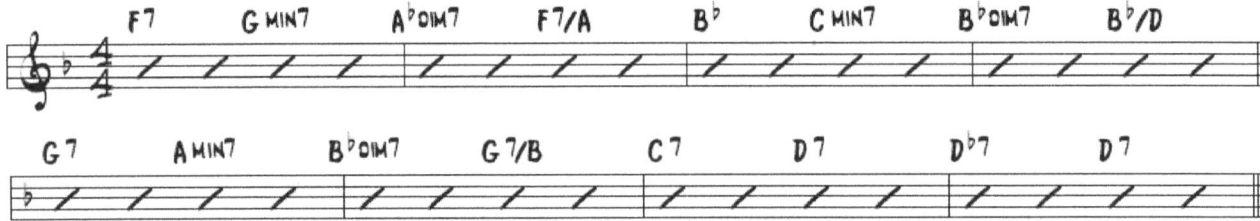

The only chords you haven't seen and won't find in Appendix A are the F7/A in the second measure, the B♭/D in the fourth measure, and the G7/B in the sixth measure. Here are the grids for those chords.

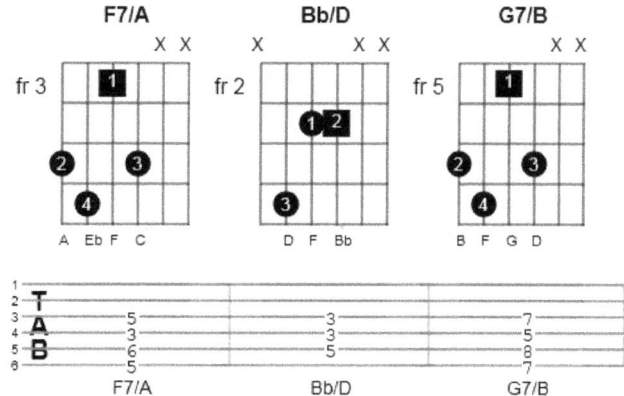

The chord forms for the first three chords should put the root of each on string 6. The fourth chord is an F7, but the bass note is A, also on string 6, which continues the ascending walking bass line. The second four chords follow the same pattern except beginning on B♭ and using string 5 for the roots. The effect is a bass line beginning on F in an F7 chord and walking upwards to D in a B♭ chord. The next four chords go from G to B in a similar walk. The last four chords end the journey with a turnaround that gets the tune back to its A part, which begins on Gmin7.

If the band includes a bass player you might want to play other forms for these chords just to stay out of the way. If you're playing solo or in sole accompaniment of your own or someone else's vocals, you can play the bass line, and it will enhance the performance. You might even try playing the stride pattern with the bass note preceding the chordal part by half a beat. *Oomph-chuck, oomph-chuck...*

Endings

These are ways that you end a tune, not to be confused with band chart repeat ending notation (Chapter 19).

The end of a tune's performance is not necessarily part of the original composition but instead something to be determined by the arranger or the performers themselves.

Endings should bring the tune's performance to a climatic conclusion in a way that satisfies listeners and lets them know the tune has ended. In show tunes as performed theatrically, there are *big* endings and *little* endings, which means the tune goes out with a bang or kind of trails off. This depends on the mood of the story being told and the nature of the tune itself. *There's No Business Like Show Business* typically has a loud, flashy ending. *Send in the Clowns* might end in a more subdued manner.

A trend developed in the 1950s to have vocal recordings of pop tunes repeat the last phrase several times as the audio faded out. That worked for when we listened to records and the radio, but it always seemed awkward when artists lip-synced their hit recordings on TV. The audio faded out, but the vocalist didn't. They just stood there looking uncomfortable.

Short Endings

The next several endings use *rhythmic notation* (Chapter 18) in the last measure to indicate coming to the end. It might not always be that way. Some bands might sustain the last note. Get together and agree on how you'll do it. After you've played together for a while, you'll hear it coming.

Generic Ending

A tune ending on its tonic for two measures often substitutes the tonic (I) and subdominant minor 7 (iv7) in the first ot the two measures. Here's how that goes in the key of C.

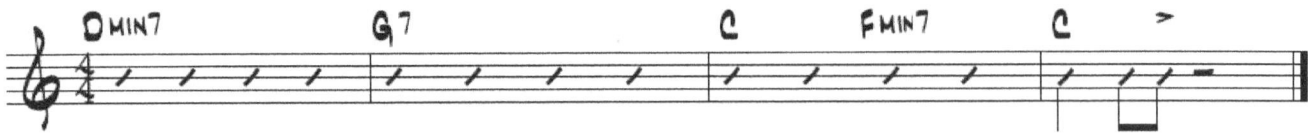

The ending shown here would be the last four measures in many tunes. It's very common and if you are ready for it and listening, you'll play it automatically.

+Five Major Seven Ending

A variation of the generic ending changes the two chords before the closing tonic chord to a major 7 chord of the augmented fifth note, in this case in the key of C, an A♭maj7.

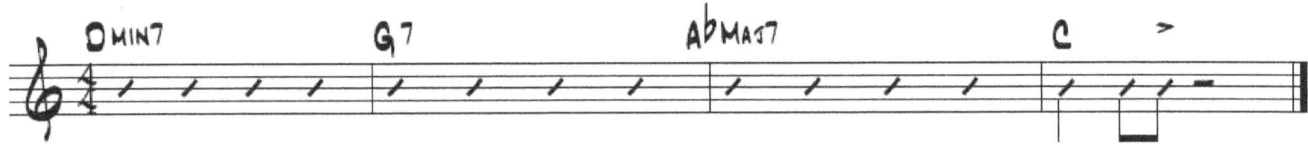

This ending works well with ballads.

A variation on that ending puts a D♭maj7 in the second two beats of the next-to-last measure, giving the ending the properties of a tri-tone substitution resolution (Chapter 16).

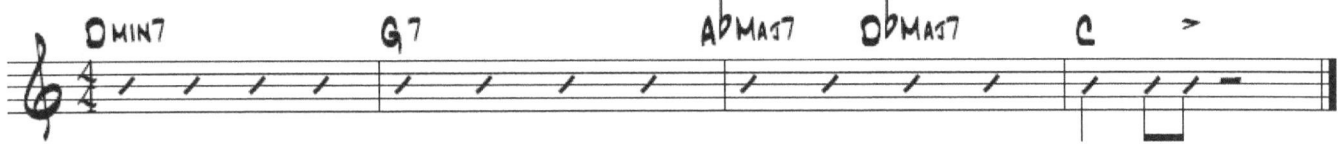

These two endings work because the last melody note, the root of the key signature's tonic chord, C in this example, is the third of the A♭maj7 chord and the major 7th of the D♭maj7 chord. You have to be careful when you use either of these. Make sure the vocalist or instrumentalist is going to sing or sing or play a C (in this example). They have been known to warble a 3rd or 5th of the tonic chord and sometimes a 9th, 6th, or even a flatted 5th just to sound hip. Any of these melodic substitutions can clash with your ending. Work it out in advance. Or wait until you hear the last melody note before you choose an ending.

Long Endings

The two-measure endings just shown are so-called *short* endings. A short ending occupies the same number of measures as would the ending of any chorus in the tune that was not the *out* (last) chorus.

The endings themselves are two measures, the last two. The examples show the preceding two measures to show you how to fit the endings into the tune.

The endings that follow are *long* endings. They take four measures.

Descending Bass

Here's a long ending in C that begins on the tonic and descends to the flat seven and then proceeds downward chromatically two beats at a time until it gets to the V dominant 7 chord.

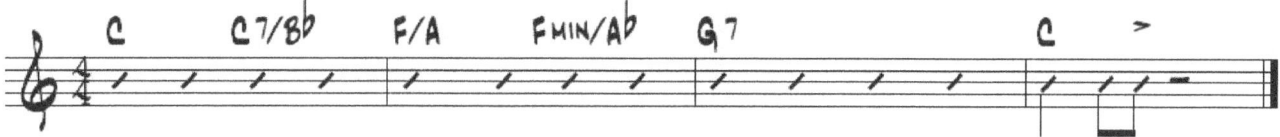

The bass line walks down from C to B♭ then A, A♭ and lands on G for a measure to resolve to the tonic C.

This example is of the ending itself. It replaces the last two measures of the tune.

Ascending Bass

Swing tunes often end with a four measure passage that walks the bass from the tonic up to the fifth like this variation on the long ending.

The bass line walks C, E, G, F#, G and finishes with C. The chord chart shows the chords you'd play to match the ending. For these long endings, we've omitted the two measures that lead into the ending. The C chord in the first measure shown above aligns with the last note in the tune, which a singer will typically hold until you get to that last measure.

Descending Bass from Flatted 5th

Bass players love this long ending. When they want you and the piano player to play it, they'll lean over and hit the first note with authority. I don't know why they do that but they always do. The descending notes begin on the flatted fifth of the signature key's tonic—F# in this case since we're in the key of C—and descend chromatically through F, E, E♭, D, D♭, and land on C, the root note of the signature key's tonic.

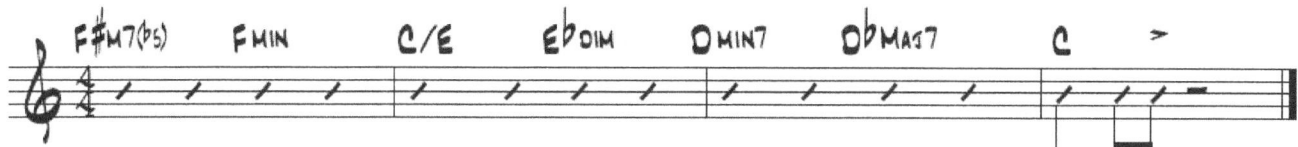

Be ready for this. You might be expecting to play the signature key's tonic chord. When you hear that big fat flatted fifth just go along with it.

Repeated Last Phrase

In this ending the last phrase of the tune up to but not including the ending is repeated twice.

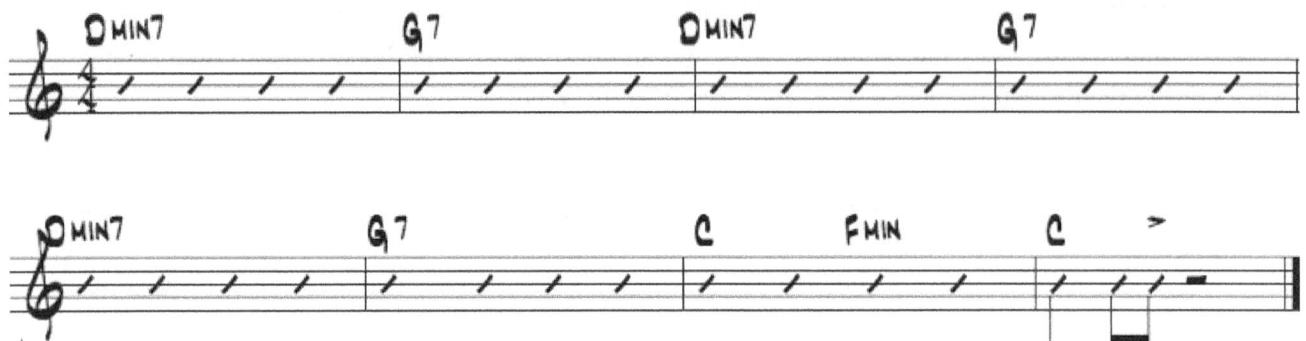

After the repeated phrase, the ending comes in. The ending after the repetitions can be long or short.

Tag

A *tag* is a special kind of long ending that extends the last chorus. It begins where the tune would normally end, with the last two measures. Instead of playing the short ending shown above, the tag substitutes a III7 to VI7 progression. In C that would be E7 to A7. Then it repeats the two measures ahead of the two it replaced followed by whichever short or long ending you would otherwise have played. Here's the final A part of a tune in C with a tag and a short ending.

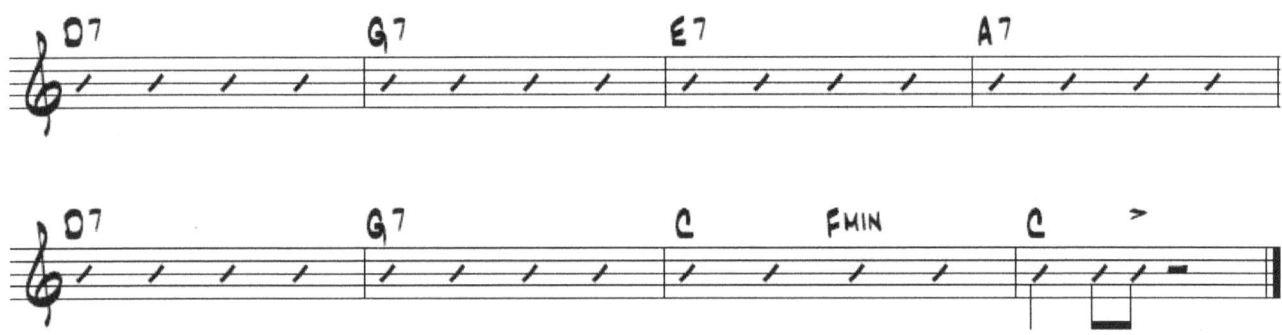

The third and fourth measures are the tag. You can see that if you delete the tag and the two measures that precede it, you get a tune with just a short ending.

You can add a long ending to a tag as well.

There are variations of how the tag gets from what would have been the tonic to the VI7 chord (A7 in this example). Sometimes you'll hit the tonic chord as a I7 and descend chromatically with dominant 7 chords to the VI7.

Dixieland Ending

The typical Dixieland band ends most of its warhorse uptempo tunes with a standard ending. It begins with a short ending just as we've seen above. Then the drums play a four-bar solo—Chapter 19 explains that four measure rest—during which time the rest of the band lays out. Then the band repeats the last four measures of the tune:

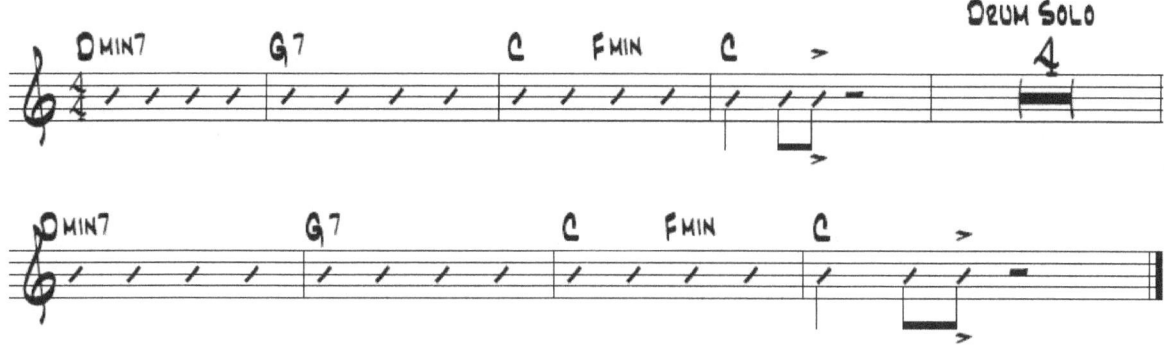

Sometimes the leader calls for a "last eight" ending, which means that after the tour bar drum solo, you play the chorus's final eight bars to the short ending.

One More Ending

Look at the last measure of all the endings in this discussion. They have the tonic chord hit with a rhythmic pattern of a quarter note and two eighth notes (Chapter 18) with the last note being short.

Now consider this variation of that measure. Again we'll use the last four measures to make our point.

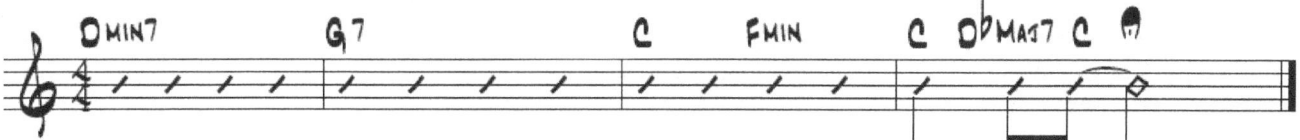

We're mainly interested in the last measure here. You can substitute it for the last measure on any of the endings in this chapter. The two-beat tonic chord and the hit on the third note of the other endings are replaced with a tonic chord, a tri-tone substitution of the V7 chord (D♭maj7 in this example), and the tonic chord held sustained for the rest of the measure. That bird's eye symbol (a *fermata*, Chapter 19) above the note means to sustain (hold for an unspecified length of time) the chord. This idiom allows the vocalist or instrumentalist to do the same or to improvise a *coda* (a line of notes that wrap around the tonic's root and closes out the tune.)

There's usually a drum hit when the sustained chord is done.

Chapter 16. Substitutions

Chapter 9 explains how to substitute colorful chords (6, maj7, 9, and 13) for their vanilla major and minor counterparts. Now we address a more advanced kind of substitution, the reharmonization of the strains in a tune.

This chapter does not provide comprehensive coverage of such substitutions. You learn only a few of them here to discover the potential for such reharmonizations. Jazz musicians call such substitutions the *hip changes*.

You can skip all this and still play effective rhythm guitar accompaniments by using standard changes. But I urge you to delve into it all. These are the harmonic enhancements that so-called *progressive jazz* players discovered in the middle of the 20th century and that have driven the advancement of jazz theories ever since.

If you're playing in a group, you have to coordinate these substitutions with the other players, particularly the piano and bass players. And you should learn to recognize them when you hear the other players use them, a collaboration that often comes intuitively after you've been working together for a while.

Just because a substitution is hip doesn't mean you should use it every time. Certainly you coordinate chord changes for recordings. They live forever and their clams and train wrecks can never be forgotten. On the bandstand, particularly in jams, just listen and don't go off on a tangent with some off-the-wall substitution that nobody ever heard of.

This chapter touches on only a few such substitutions, the blues variations and tritone substitutions being the most prevalent.

The Blues Redux

Chapter 13 taught you the fundamental chord changes for the twelve-bar blues. Now you'll learn some alternative blues changes that have come into widespread use among jazz musicians. We'll keep it all in the key of G, a favorite among guitar players.

For review and reference, here are the basic blues changes you learned in Chapter 13:

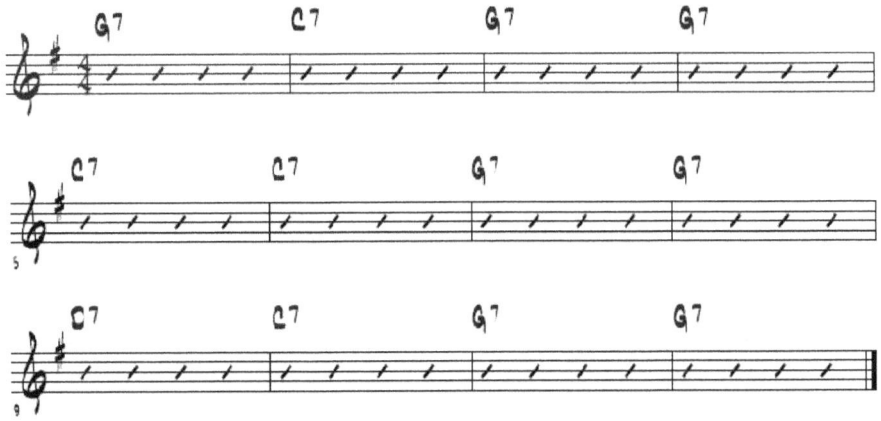

Nothing's changed about the blues since then, but some things are about to.

Blues Substitution #1 (*de facto*)

The first set of substitutions is common and is shown here. Unless you are in a rock band, chances are the bass player will play these changes without giving it a second thought. These have become the *de facto* standard changes for jazz-oriented blues.

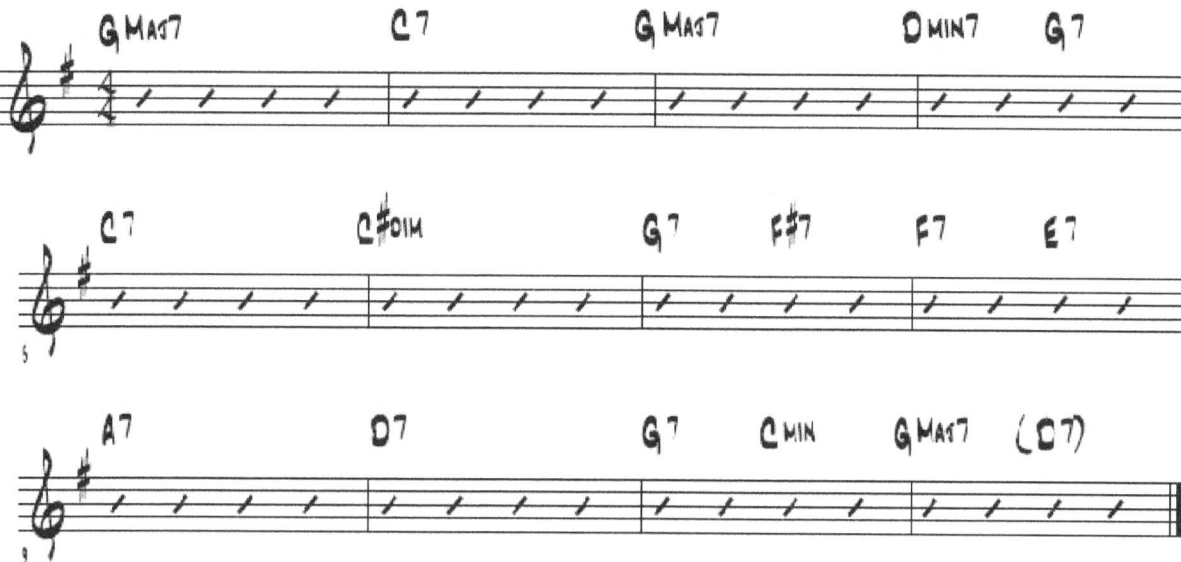

The first change you see when comparing these blues to those in the original changes is that the first chord is Gmaj7. Then, in measure 4, the G7 is replaced with Dmin7 G7. This is a common substitution for many dominant seven chords, which this chapter discusses in **Preceding Minor 7**. The C7 in measure 6 is replaced with a C#dim chord. Next, beginning in measure 7, the G7 chord begins a downward chromatic progression of F#7, F7, to land on E7. Finally, in measure 9, A7 resolves to D7 in measure 10, which resolves to G7 in measure 11. If this is the end of the performance—the last chorus—the final D7 is left out. Otherwise it leads back to measure 1 for the next chorus.

Blues Substitution #2 (*Bird changes*)

The second substitution for the blues employs the well-known "Bird" changes, named after Charlie Parker, who was known to take harmonic liberties with the tunes he played.

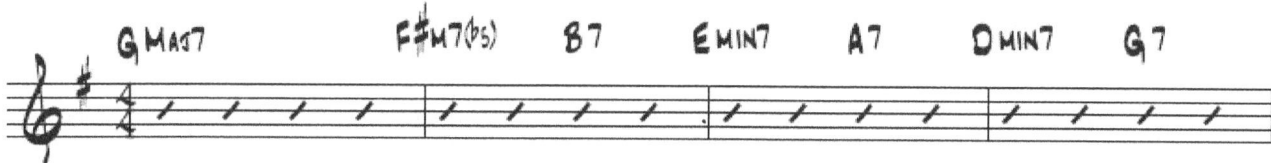

We need look only at the first four measures for this substitution. The rest of the changes are standard blues. One thing most blues changes have in common is that they begin with the tonic in measure one (Gmaj7 in this case) and resolve to the tonic dominant 7 in measure 4 (G7 in this case). The various substitutions or variations have to do with how the changes get there. In this substitution, the second measure moves down a half tone from the tonic and plays three measures of the cycle of fourths, two beats to the chord. It varies between minor 7 and dominant 7 as it travels the cycle, ending on the G7 which was the objective from the start.

There are many other blues substitutions. If you know these two in all the jazz keys, you are well prepared to hold forth at the local jam. You'll encounter others in band and chord charts and lead sheets as you expand your jazz repertoire. Each time you find a new one, put it to use and make it part of your jazz vocabulary.

Exercise: Play the blues with both substitutions in G over and over. Get other cats to jam with you.

Exercise: Transpose the blues to B♭, C, E♭ and F. Jam on those changes too.

Preceding Minor 7

Let's return to the Sears Roebuck bridge that Chapter 15 addressed.

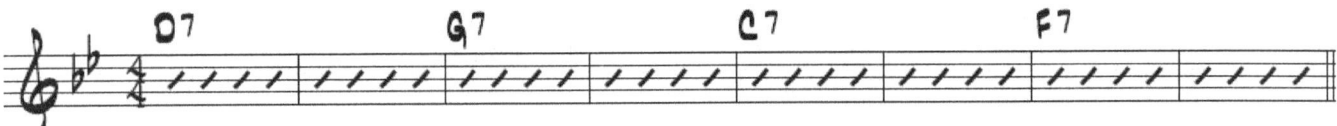

Because each chord takes two measures, players often precede each dominant 7 chord with the minor 7 that resolves to it. We'll switch from the key of B♭ to the key of C just for some variety. With these substitution the Sears Roebuck bridge in the key of C would look like this.

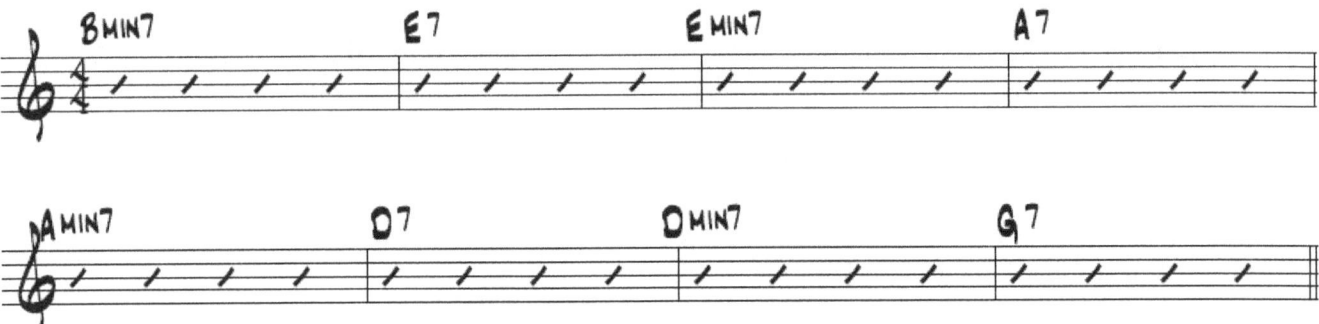

A jazz piano teacher once taught me that every dominant 7 chord can and should be preceded with the minor 7 chord that resolves to it. He said it always fits irrespective of the melody. It gives the changes a suspended feel for, in this case, four beats. He was right. I don't always insert the minor 7 chord like he did religiously. Whenever I do, it always fits.

Tritone Substitution

The *tritone substitution* is the best known and most often used jazz substitution. It's a hip-sounding substitution of one chord where a different one is expected, specifically, of the chord that is three tones away from the original one.

What's a *tritone*? It's what its name implies. It's an interval three full tones away. For example, the tritone of C is F#. Count the whole tone intervals between the two. C, D, E, F#. You move upward three whole tones—a tritone—to get there. If you move downward, C, B♭, A♭, F#, it's the same number of tones.

It follows that since C's tritone is F#, F#'s tritone is C. The same relationship exists between all six tritone pairs in the twelve-tone scale. Here they are:

C, F#
Db, G
D, Ab
Eb, A
E, Bb
F, B

Now consider the harmonic properties of a dominant 7 chord. C7, for example, resolves to F in the cycle of fifths/fourths (Chapter 8). It is harmonically pleasing to allow F# to resolve to F as well, since F is a half step down.

Exercise: Play these chords on your guitar. C7, F and then F#7, F.

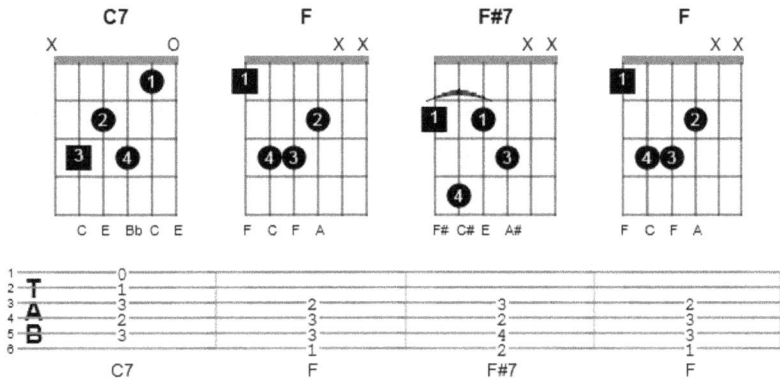

You'll hear the similarity. Both dominant 7 chords, tritones of each other, readily resolve to the same major chord.

It then follows that if Gmin7, C7, F sounds good—see **Preceding minor 7** above—you can insert F#'s preceding minor 7 chord in the substitution, by playing Dbmin7, F#7, F. Why does this work? Because Db and G are tritones to one another, and Dbmin7 resolves to F#7.

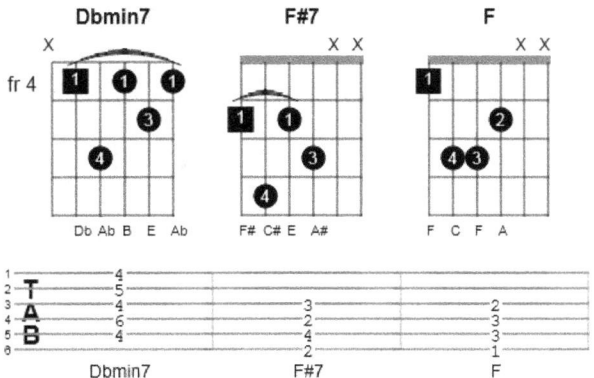

Exercise: Play these three forms in successions up and down the fretboard, saying the names of the chord symbols as you play.

The tritone has other applications for hip substitutions. Players tend to call it the *flatted fifth* substitution because tritones are also the flatted fifths of each other. We'll explore some of that next.

Flatted Fifth Descent

Like the tritone substitution for dominant 7 chords, the flatted fifth descent is widely known and popular among musicians. It's often used as an ending (Chapter 15), but it works well at phrases that normally begin on the tonic and proceed one way or another to the ii7 chord. Consider many pop standards with A part beginnings harmonized this way to get from the tonic to the V7 chord in four measures:

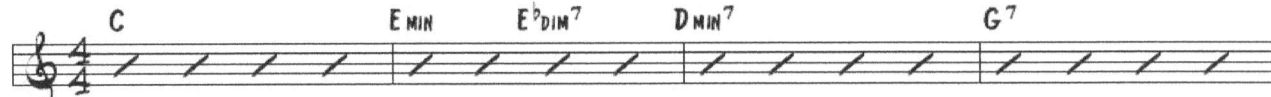

Here's the same progression but with the flatted fifth descent substituted in the first measure:

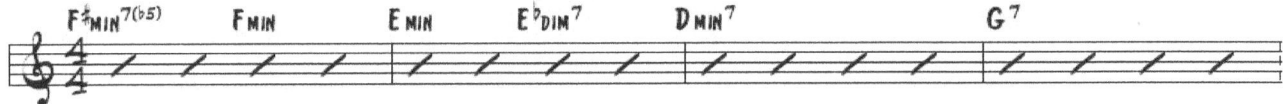

This version of the flatted fifth descent substitution substitutes itself for the tonic chord rather than for a dominant 7, and its tritone chord is half-diminished to accommodate the melody.

Alternative Reharmonizations

These are the hip changes that musicians often substitute for the originals. In some cases, the hip changes have become *de facto* standard changes, and the original ones are forgotten or at least discarded. Several of Hoagy Carmichael's tunes—*Skylark*, *Stardust*, and *Georgia on my Mind*, for example—have been reharmonized by jazz players. If you could ask them—if they were still alive—they'd say they "fixed" the tunes.

Often, a reharmonization happened because sheet music publishers of yore dumbed down piano arrangements to make them easier for amateur pianists, guitarists and ukulele strummers. The easy chords weren't always the best choices, and the jazz players were quick to correct the problem.

We'll look at passages from two ballads in which the changes have been rewritten for a more pleasing—to the jazz player's ear—sound. You can compare the originals with the updated versions to see which you prefer. As with most substitutions, you should coordinate their choice with the other players in your ensemble.

"Someone to Watch Over Me"

George Gershwin wrote *Someone to Watch Over Me* in 1926 and it was to become a timeless standard recorded by pop and jazz musicians countless times.

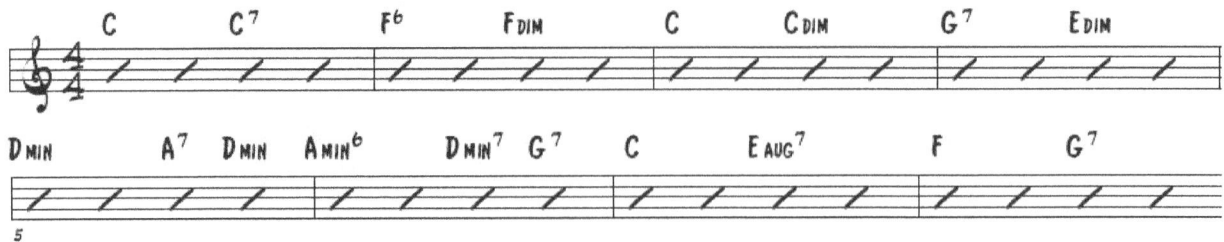

In the 1950s, pianist Art Tatum recorded *Someone to Watch Over Me* and introduced harmonic substitutions that essentially redefined the tune. Musicians have been using these alternative changes ever since.

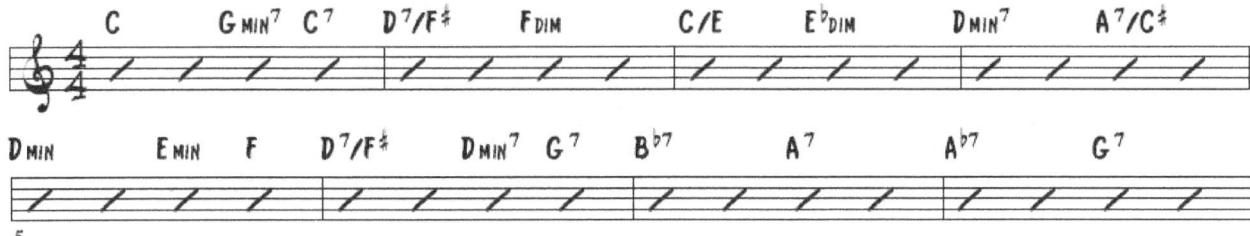

Tatum's changes are a study in the use of harmonic substitutions to insert lines—chromatic descents and ascents—as counter melodies. In the second measure he begins with an F# that then descends chromatically over the next two measures to land on the C# that is the 3rd of the A7 chord. Then in the fifth measure he heads back up the chromatic scale from D to F# on the first beat in measure 6. After that he ends the first eight measures with a substitution for the 1-6-2-5 (Chapter 12) turnaround (Chapter 15) with another chromatic descent from B♭ to G.

Tatum's interpretation also changes how the bridge is harmonized. I'll leave that to you to research.

"I Can't Get Started With You"

This is the original version of *I Can't Get Started With You* as penned by Vernon Duke. It has been recorded countless times with these changes as the preferred ones.

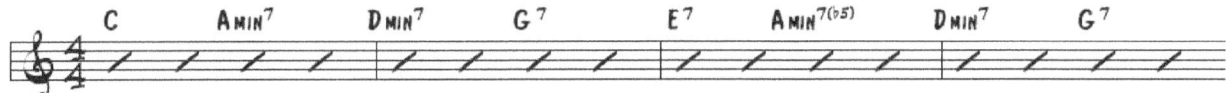

Sometime during the be-bop era, someone crafted these alternative changes, and they have become the ones of choice by many jazz musicians.

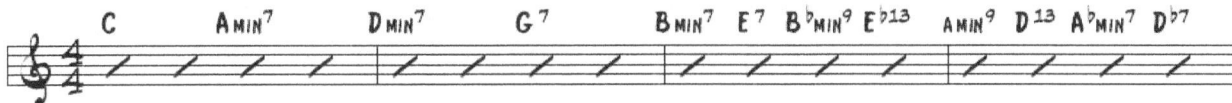

The substitution runs a two-chord minor 7 to dominant 7 sequence descending one-half tone at a time. The two final chords in that descent, A♭min7 to D♭7, is the tritone substitution for the original version's G7, both of which resolve to the C in the next measure (not shown here).

PART V. Charts

Are you ready to read some music? Don't know how? Don't worry, you don't have to learn everything there is to know about scores. But there are some basics that will come in handy when you get together with other musicians and somebody pulls out an arrangement or a fake book. And, of course, reading is a required skill when you play in a big band. This Part explains as much of all that you'll need in order to get started.

Chapter 17. Chord Charts

We've seen chord charts earlier as we learned about parts of the tunes. Now we'll learn about the charts themselves. Don't skip this chapter. You are assumed in the next two chapters to know the concepts and chart components explained here. If you think you already know them, read it anyway so we're speaking the same language later.

To begin, here is the complete chord chart for the old jazz standard, *After You've Gone*.

After You've Gone was originally written and played in two-beat, which was the popular dance idiom in 1918 when it was written and first became popular. Jazz players adopted it, sped it up, doubled its time to four-beat, and it became a standard.

This chart uses slash notation (Chapter 5) except for the last measure which uses rhythmic notation (Chapters 5 and 17). You might be given a similar chart with melody notes in keyboard notation. That would be a lead sheet, and, unless you're playing a melodic solo (Chapter 22), you can ignore the notes and assume slash notation, four beats to the measure.

The chords are simple—you've already seen some of them in this book.

The chart shown here is the complete tune, one chorus. It does not include intros, turnarounds, endings, or any other kind of additional passages (Chapter 15) other than what are part of the tune itself. You will be expected to play from this chart with as many choruses as the performance and the configuration of your group demands. If it's a combo, you'll play the head once or twice, then you will accompany solos by the individual players, which might include you if you are up to it. The only time you lay out completely is during a drum solo or some other special head arrangement called out at the time. For example, a sax player might want to play with bass only with the rest of the rhythm section laying out.

The chart is the tune itself. How you play it, how many choruses, and so on, are specified at the moment. The chart simply tells you what chords to play during each chorus.

You might be expected to provide a dominant 7 chord in the last measure to resolve back to the top for each of the choruses except the last one. You might be expected to play a canned ending (Chapter 15) at the end of the last chorus.

After You've Gone begins on the IV chord instead of the tonic, so your chord getting back to the top would be I7, B♭7 in this case.

Whatever is expected of you, this chart is not an arrangement; it's not even a road map. All of that exists in the heads of the players at the time of the performance.

Title

The title is at the top of the chart. You recognize that.

Staves

Each row of five horizontal lines is a *staff*. Each staff section divided by vertical lines is a *measure* also called a *bar*. The vertical lines are *barlines*. The chord symbols are above the staves (plural of staff) they are to be played in. Those are the chords you learned about in Chapter 4.

This chart consists of ten staves of four measures each. Most chord charts will be thirty-two measures. *After You've Gone* does not follow the AABA format and thus has forty measures. Each measure has four beats as you can see.

Clef Sign

That funny looking backward S symbol at the beginning of each staff tells the player that they should read the *treble clef*. Don't worry about that if you don't know what it means. Clefs are meaningless in a chord chart because chords can be played on any clef.

Key Signature

The cluster of three little ♭ symbols to the right of the clef sign in the first staff is the *key signature*. It tells you what key the tune is in, in this case, E♭. Again, it's helpful to know that, but it isn't absolutely necessary. You're given all the chord symbols, and the key signature should not affect how you play them.

Time Signature

The 4 over 4 symbol to the right of the key signature is the *time signature*. The top 4 means that there are four beats to the measure. The lower 4 specifies that each quarter note gets a beat, something that you don't need to worry about when reading chord sheets. You'll need to know it later. The time signature does not repeat on successive staves. It will, however, be included if the time changes, something that doesn't happen in mainstream jazz (or shouldn't).

Note that a waltz will specify 3 over 4, meaning three beats to the measure in which case you should expect each measure to have three instead of four slashes.

There are other time signatures. *Take Five* is five beats to the measure. Other than for that one, unless you are playing Dave Brubeck standards, you won't have to worry about them. If you are called upon to read a chord chart on *Take Five* expect five slashes and play them like 1-2-3-1-2.

Measures

The tiny digits under the first measure of each staff is the measure number, which you use to discuss the chart with other players.

Note that measures 16 and 24 have a double vertical line separating them from their next measure. This tells you in this case where a new passage (Chapter 15) begins and ends. That's handy for when you get lost, but not all charts use the convention. In AABA tunes, the double lines identify where the B part, the bridge, begins and ends.

Tempo

Note that the chart has a tempo indication above the first staff's first measure. That indication simply says "Ballad" but it can specify how many beats to the minute or it might simply say something meaningful about the tune: "slow," "medium," and so on. Don't worry about it. If you know the tune, you'll know how fast or slow it should be played. Otherwise, the leader or the vocalist or instrumentalist you are accompanying will kick off the tempo.

Chapter 18. Rhythmic Notation

Rhythmic notation uses the chord chart format but adds note-like symbols to describe the rhythm patterns that the rhythm section is expected to play. This depiction is common in big band charts. You'll see the same rhythmic patterns on the drum and piano parts and often the trumpet parts too, although they'll have specific notes to play. We'll discuss this further in Chapter 19.

Look back at the *After You've Gone* chord chart in Chapter 17, which is mostly slash notation. Following is a new old song in traditional AABA format that also uses slash notation but with places where rhythms are specified.

I wrote this song when I was a teenager. My best friend sang it in a high school talent show to my accompaniment. I dedicated it to a girl I was interested in. She was embarrassed at being called out publicly by the school nerd and never spoke to me again.

Pay attention to measures 7 and 8, 15 and 16, 24, and 32. All the other measures use slash notation, which means you strum four to the bar. But those measures have note-like symbols and rests. Each symbol represents a beat, a portion of a beat, or more than one beat. How much depends on the note symbol's shape.

There's much more to rhythmic notation than you will learn here, but this much will get you started. If you are playing in a session where precision is required, the other players will correct you if you mess some-

teach yourself Rhythm Jazz Guitar, *a player's guide* – Al Stevens

thing up. Eventually with experience, you'll reach a point where when you look at a measure or several measures of rhythmic notation, you know how the rhythms work.

This chart is in 4/4 time, which means there are four beats to each measure and a quarter note gets a beat. That's all you need to know about time signatures for now. As a jazz player you will sometimes play in 3/4 time and very rarely in 5/4 time.

The following chart specifies the shape and beat value of each of the rhythmic notation note and rest symbols. It gets a lot deeper than this for melodic and harmonic parts, but these are about all you'll see in guitar accompaniment charts.

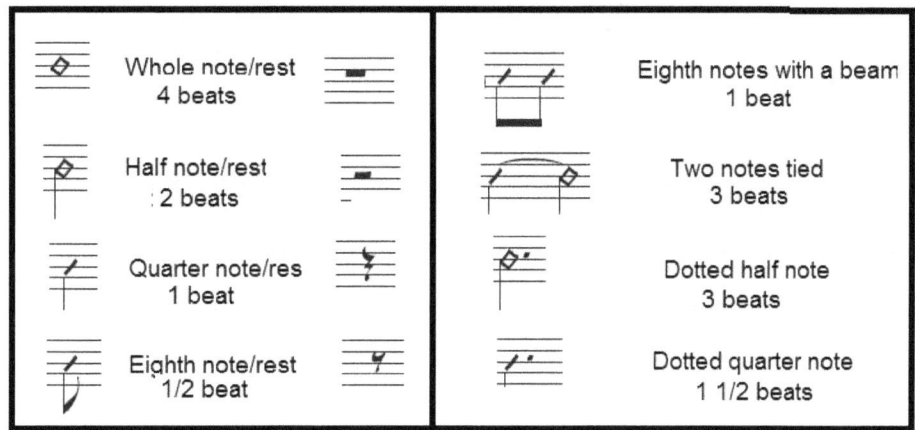

To put this notation into context, you have to start at the beginning. We won't do that here; there are many tutorials available to teach you to read music. For now, consider this small example.

Count this off following the beat numbers under the staff. Think, *one and two and three and four* for each measure

The first note gets two beats. The second and third notes get one beat each. That's the first measure.

The first note in the second measure is an eighth note which gets a half beat. That means the second note in that measure starts a half-beat ahead of the second beat on the first "and" and is a quarter note that lasts the value of a beat, so it lasts until the second half of the second beat on the second "and".

The third note in the second measure is an eighth note, so the first three notes in the second measure equal two beats although only the first one is sounded on a beat. The last note in that measure is another half note that finishes the measure.

Got all that? Great. Here's a trick. Read the notation, speaking the lyrics in a meter that matches the rhythms.

"Hey, you there, who parked the car?"

The next time you see an eighth-quarter-eighth string of notes followed by another note, "who parked the car" will pop into your head. Eventually all the rhythmic patterns you'll ever see you will have seen countless times, and you'll know what they sound like without having to hear them first.

This small treatment is just an introduction, an overview, a sneak preview of reading music. To sight read a full chart takes lots of practice. Imagine having to combine that with note values to play melodies and harmonies. That's what your colleagues in the big bands have to do. Of course, you have to combine these beat values with the chord symbols above them, not shown in the example, but that are on all the chord charts.

Chapter 19. Big Band Charts

Reading band charts is another of those skills that takes lots of practice to master. It gets easier as you progress. If you play in a big band, you'll get to read a fixed set of arrangements, the band's standards. Every band plays *In the Mood*, for example. Your band will have its own set of other standard tunes as well, usually favorites that your audiences recognize and like to dance to.

From reading those arrangements, you'll come to recognize the notations that tell you what to play and when. Eventually you'll be able to sight-read charts you've never seen before.

That's your goal as a big band guitar player. Studio playing needs musicians who can read the charts on sight without consuming expensive studio time and the time of the other musicians learning what's on the chart. I recommend finding a local community big hand that needs a guitar player, maybe just a relief guitar player. If you can do everything this book teaches, they'll be looking for you.

This chapter is an overview. If you run into notation that isn't explained—and there is a lot more to it than we show here—ask one of your fellow musicians about it. To understand this discussion, you must already know what is presented in Chapters 16 and 17. A review of those chapters might be helpful before you get into this one.

You have two kinds of notational symbols to watch for besides the ones that specify chords and rhythms. These two categories are *navigation* and *interpretation* chart symbols also called *markings*.

The chart for *A Place Called Nowhere*, shown below, contains elements you'll need to understand on the guitar part for big band arrangements. Once you have them under your belt, you'll be ready to take on the real thing.

It might look cryptic and esoteric and it is. But you'll learn what it all means with practice.

The most frequent problem experienced by reading newcomers is keeping their place in the chart and not getting lost.

You already learned to read simple chord charts (Chapters 16 and 17) that lay down the changes and rhythmic patterns for one chorus of a tune. Big band charts have all that plus other markings that tell you when to play what, where to go next on the chart, and small subtleties, such as dynamic and expression markings.

A Chart to Study

This chapter gives an overview of each of the markings on such charts. We use an arrangement of a tune I wrote called *A Place Called Nowhere*. You'll find a backing track for the tune at http://www.alstevens.com/jazzguitar so you can hear the lyrics and melody.

teach yourself Rhythm Jazz Guitar, *a player's guide* – Al Stevens

It might be helpful to print this chart so you can highlight the various elements as we discuss them. If you cannot print from this book, you can download a PDF of the chart from http://www.alstevens.com/jazzguitar/.

Now let's look at *A Place Called Nowhere* piece by piece.

Rehearsal Numbers

There are two uppercase letters inside circles, one at measure 5 and the other at measure 13. These are called *rehearsal numbers* even though they aren't really numerical digits. Some arrangements will indeed have numbers. Some will be boxed rather than in circles. Some leaders will say "circle one," "circle two," and so on, whether they're in boxes, circles, or whatever. Their purpose is to provide ways to address specific locations in the arrangement when you and the other players discuss it. They have no bearing on the chart's playing or your navigation of it.

Navigation

Navigation is important to any journey. It keeps you from getting lost. That's why the navigation markings on an arrangement are often called a *road map*.

When I see a big band chart for the first time, my first task is to eyeball it beginning to end, making a mental note of where the navigational markings are so that when I get to a mark that jumps the arrangement to another place in the chart, maybe several pages away, forward or backward, I am not surprised. I already know where that destination is on the chart.

A yellow highlighting pen is helpful, but get permission first. The band's librarian might not want you marking up the pages.

> *I was pianist with the Tommy Dorsey Orchestra for a couple years, and we used the same paper chart copies that the original band used in the 1930s, 40s, and 50s. They had an antique value to my traditional thinking, so, out of respect for their antiquity, I used small Post-it notes stuck to the margins to mark where things were.*

The chart consists of a four-measure intro (Chapter 15), the chorus played twice, and a tag with a long ending (Chapter 15). Finding your way from the beginning to the end of the arrangement requires you to read and correctly interpret the navigation markings.

This chart has measure numbers at the beginning of each staff. We can use them to reference the markings.

Repeat Signs

These two markings, the first at measure 5 and the second at measure 20, are left and right *repeat signs* that mark a passage that is to be played more than once.

The first time you encounter the left repeat sign, you pass it by. Don't ignore it, though. Remember where it is, because when you come to the right repeat sign, you return to the measure that follows the left repeat sign, and in a complex big band chart, that can be several pages back. If there is no left repeat sign, you return to the beginning of the passage marked by the nearest double bar or if there is no double bar, the beginning of the arrangement.

Endings

These markings mark the endings of repeated passages. You play the first ending, the one numbered 1 at measure 17, the first time you play the passage. When you reach the right repeat sign at measure 20, you return to the left repeat sign at measure 5 and play the passage a second time. This time, when you get to the first ending at measure 17, you jump over it to the second ending at measure 21 and play that.

This arrangement uses only two endings for its one repeated passage, but there can be endings, 3, 4, and so on, and there can be multiple repeated passages and endings in an arrangement.

Segno

Segno is Italian for *sign*. Most musicians call it by its English name.

The sign marks a place in the chart where the arrangement will return to resume playing. In the chart above, it's at measure 5 along with the rehearsal number A and the left repeat sign. Don't confuse the two signs. The left repeat sign needs a right repeat sign paired with it to tell you when to return, and, of course, they need to be in logical proximity to one another so there's no question about where to return to. The sign, however can be returned to from anywhere later in the arrangement as explained next in the discussion of **D.S. al Coda**.

D.S. al Coda

The **D.S. al Coda** marking (measure 24) directs you to return to the sign (measure 5) and proceed playing until you arrive at the **Coda** marking (measure 22).

D.C. al Coda

The **D.C. al Coda** marking (not on the example chart) directs you to return to the beginning of the arrangement, the very first measure.

Coda

The **Coda** marking at measure 22 tells you to complete that measure and jump to what is called the *Coda*, which begins at measure 25.

You make the jump only if you are at the coda sign following the D.S. al Coda or D.C. al Coda. Otherwise, you past it by, although you should take note of where it is for the next time through.

Sometimes the first **Coda** marking is replaced with text that says, **to Coda**.

The second **Coda** (measure 25 in the example) marks the beginning of the last passage in the arrangement. Most times.

Repeated Measures

Measures 28 contains a marking that tells you to repeat the previous measure.

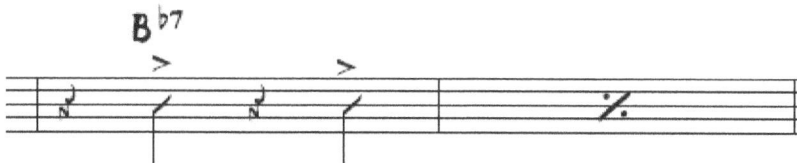

You would play the chord and rhythms in measure 27 a second time.

Multi-measure Rests

Measures 1 through 4 are represented by this marking:

This is a *multi-measure rest.* You will lay out (rest, remain tacit) for the number of measures noted in the marking, four in this case. Just sit quietly and count.

Speaking of that, it is considered bad form to count in such a visible manner that the audience can tell that's what you're doing. It's okay to tap your foot and count mentally, but don't mouth the words of the numbers you are counting. "**One**, two, three, four, **two**, two three, four..." Don't do that. It identifies you as an amateur. Don't count on your fingers, either.

Interpretation

Up to now you've learned how to identify and form your chords, when to play them, and how to find your way around a chart. Now you'll get into the more subtle, the more sensitive aspects of reading. Every piece of music is subject to the interpretation of the musician with respect to tempo, volume, attack, and so on. But arrangements have written clues as to how the arranger wants you to interpret the work, to insert his or her own interpretation and to keep all the musicians in the ensemble on the same track.

These markings specify the arranger's intentions with respect to dynamics and articulation.

Dynamics

The *dynamics* markings of a musical note, measure, passage, and the tune itself denote how loudly or softly you are to play at various places in the performance. These are the most-often ignored markings in band charts. Band members can get so wrapped up in playing the notes and being heard that they overlook one of the most sensitive aspects of musical interpretations. The trumpet section is usually too loud, the piano too soft, the guitar player gets carried away with his or her amp, and so on.

A famous conductor was invited to appear as guest conductor for a prominent concert orchestra. He arrived on time for the dress rehearsal to make his first appearance on that particular podium. The musicians welcomed him in anticipation of his appearance. He stood at the podium and looked around at the eager faces. He raised his baton and held it up for a moment. Then he said to the orchestra, "Too loud."

Dynamic Levels

The dynamic level markings shown below specify the volume to be played beginning at the measure where the marking appears. Following are the markings, their Italian names, and what they mean.

pp	*pianissimo*	very soft
p	*piano*	soft
mp	*mezzo piano*	medium soft
mf	*mezzo forte*	medium loud
f	*forte*	loud
ff	*fortissimo*	very loud

Measures 5, 13, and 17 in the example chart have dynamic markings.

There are also **ppp** and **fff**, at which point it gets ridiculous for a big band.

How loud is very loud, how soft is very soft, and everything in between? It's really a matter of interpretation by the individual musician and the band. As long as you agree and the music sounds right, it's right. The dynamic level changes reflect the relative difference between the loudest and the softest passages, and that audio dynamic range might vary depending on the size of the room, whether you're playing acoustic or amplified, the number of people in the audience, and whether they're noisy (like in a bar) or attentive (like in an auditorium).

*As the story goes, when jazz legend Louis Armstrong joined his first big band, he needed to learn the rudiments of reading music. In a rehearsal, the band was into a quiet passage and everyone was playing softly. Everyone except Satch, that is. He was taking the paint off the back walls with his trumpet. The leader stopped the tune and asked why Louis was playing so loudly. He said he saw the **pp** dynamic marking and thought it meant "pound plenty."*

Diminuendo and Crescendo

When the chart wants you to get quieter or louder, it will include *crescendo* and *diminuendo* marks as shown here in measures 12 and 16 of the example chart.

The measures that follow such markings often include dynamic level markings to indicate how much louder or more quietly you should be playing. In the example you are playing *piano* (***p***) when you get to the *crescendo* at measure 12 and measure 13 is marked *mezzo forte* (***mf***). Measure 16 with the *diminuendo* goes from *mezzo forte* (***mf***) back down to *piano* (***p***).

The *diminuendo* and *crescendo* markings can span multiple measures.

These markings convey to the musicians what the arranger wants to hear with respect to dynamics. Sometimes you have to get quieter because the arrangement wants a gentler feel. Sometimes because the band is backing a vocalist or instrumental solo or *soli*, and the background music must not drown them out. Sometimes you have to play more loudly for your part to be heard over the band itself.

Try to observe and comply with the dynamic markings in an arrangement. You'll be one of the few.

Articulation

Articulation markings specify how you are to play specific chords. They override dynamic markings for the duration of that one chord and they can override the chord's duration itself.

Staccato

A *staccato* chord is marked with a dot above or below the notehead. With the rhythmic notation of guitar charts, it's always above. But if you are reading a piano chart with keyboard notation (Chapter 5), the *staccato* dot will be below those notes that have upward-pointing stems.

A chord marked staccato is played shorter than its notation would suggest. It is usually played at half the duration.

Staccato is a shorthand way to keep charts less cluttered. Without it, the rhythmic notation in the example above would have a sixteenth note followed by a sixteenth rest. Such notation is busy and difficult to read.

Measures 20 and 26 in the example chart contain *staccato* chords.

Accent

The *accent* marking specifies that you are to play the chord somewhat louder and with more attack than its neighbors. Then, for the next chord you return to the current dynamic.

Measure 27 in the example chart contains two *accent* chords. This measure is an example of a *back beat*, in which the chords are played on beats two and four with rests on beats one and three.

Marcato

Marcato is similar to *accent* except that the volume is a bit louder and the attack is more prominent.

The example chart has no *mercato* chords, but they are often used.

Fermata

A *fermata*, also called a *birds-eye*, is placed over (or under in piano charts depending on the stem direction) a chord that is to be sustained, held longer than it normally would be based on its notation.

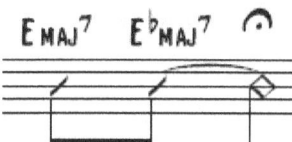

The *fermata* is often found on the last chord of ballads where an abrupt ending is not wanted. It allows vocalists and soloists to improvise an obbligato, which is a melodic line of indeterminate length inserted by a soloist.

Measure 30, the closing measure of the example chart, contains a *fermata*.

Other Articulations

There are other articulation markings, and if you encounter them, ask your buddies what they mean. Chances are the rhythm guitar's normal *staccato* strum (Chapters 2 and 19) will override whatever the arranger wrote down, particularly if the arranger does not play guitar.

Expression

About the only *expression* marking you'll see in a big band guitar chart is the RIT. mark which tells you to slow the tempo gradually. Here it is at measure 29 in the example chart.

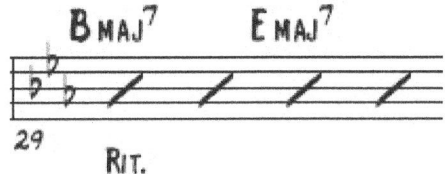

The degree of slowing is subject to the musicians' interpretation. Typically the leader will conduct the gradual tempo decrease.

Key Changes

Key changes, also called *modulations*, are not something for you to absolutely have to worry about, since you're playing chords based on their symbols rather than from musical note notation. A C7 is a C7 no matter what key you are playing in. Nevertheless, it's helpful to know what key you are in. If the arrangement changes keys, there will be a new key signature looking something like this:

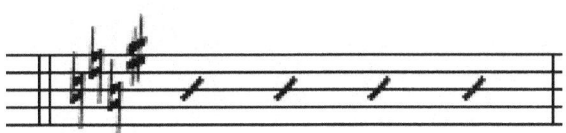

The accidentals in the key signature for the previous passage that no longer apply are marked *natural* (♮) and the new key signature follows. If some of the original signature's accidentals continue, such as when you go from E♭ (three flats) to B♭ (two flats), only the one flat is marked natural in the new signature.

Why do you care about the key signature when the chart provides the chord symbols? Knowing the tonal center of the key you are in helps your mind find its place in the arrangement and reinforces your ear playing. That doesn't happen right off the bat, but with experience, "hearing" the next chord comes naturally.

A Walk Through the Chart

Given what we know about all the markings in this chart, let's take a walk, measure by measure, through *A Place Called Nowhere* as you would play it.

1. At the top, lay out for four measures while others in the ensemble play the intro.
2. At rehearsal number A, measure 5, make note of the left repeat sign and the Segno for future reference
3. Strum quietly for seven measures.
4. At measure 12 bring the volume up slightly.
5. At rehearsal number B play a bit more loudly for three measures.
6. At measure 16, bring it back down and play more quietly.
7. Play at measure 17, which starts the first ending and play until measure 20.
8. After measure 20, return to the left repeat sign at rehearsal number A, measure 5.
9. Repeat measures 5 through 16.
10. Skip the first ending and proceed to the second ending, which begins at measure 21.
11. Play measures 21 through 24 up to and including the *D.S. al Coda* marking.

12. Return to the Segno at measure 5.
13. Iterate steps 3 through 10 above, putting you at the second ending.
14. Play measures 21 and 22 up to the Coda sign in measure 22.
15. Skip to the Coda which begins in measure 25.
16. Play through measure 28.
17. At measure 29, the *rit* mark, begin to play more slowly, gradually reducing the tempo until the end of the arrangement at measure 30.
18. At measure 30, where there is a *fermata,* sustain the last chord until the leader signals to cut it off.

Congratulations, you've just *read* your first big band chart.

Exercise: Pick up your guitar, turn on the backing track, and *play* your first big band chart.

PART VI. Playing

Part VI takes you beyond the role of rhythm guitarist but only to introduce you to the worlds of comping and improvisation. These subjects warrant books of their own, and many such books exist. But you'll have fun digging into them, getting inspired, and pushing yourself to the next level of jazz guitar.

Chapter 20. Freddie

Freddie Green is most often associated with a rhythmic style of jazz guitar in which the guitar keeps time and lays down very sparse chords. His method is effective in a band setting where you have a bass player and another chord instrument—piano, typically—filling in with the notes that the guitar does not play. But you would probably not use it to accompany a vocalist without a band.

Freddie's philosophy about rhythm guitar was that it should sound "like the drummer is playing chords." He was a staple in the rhythm section of the Count Basie band for a half century. Freddie strummed a hard four-beat rhythm accompaniment and pioneered the sound that many rhythm guitarists emulate and virtually all big-band leaders want to hear. This chapter explains elements of Freddie's style of rhythm guitar.

To begin, I suggest you get the album, *Mr. Rhythm Freddie Green*. It features Freddie as leader of a small swing band. You can hear his prominent rhythmic guitar throughout. In his other recordings—mostly with the Basie band—the guitar often can't be heard as well as we'd like. That's true of many older band recordings. The guitar is usually acoustic, and the brass and reed sections and particularly the drums drown it out. Not so with this recording. As I write this, the complete album is available on YouTube.

There are also many online videos that teach Freddie's method for rhythm guitar. Watch and learn from as many of these as you can. I won't recommend one over the others because every one I've watched has something to teach, and internet content has a way of going away without notice. Those tutorials teach many more aspects of Freddie's playing than I do here. We're only touching on the concept. There's a lot more about it for you to learn.

The essence of Freddie's playing is that he plays two- and three-note chords in a driving four-beat time pattern. He does not accent beats two and four as has been suggested. All four chords in a 4/4 measure have equal amplitude and attack. His chords typically leave out the root note and any color notes (Chapter 9). He often plays only the third and dominant or major seventh notes for the current chord. This method, of course, depends on having a bass in the band—usually an upright string bass—to lay down the bottom. Freddie gripped and released the strings with each chord causing it to sound and then go silent, leaving space between it and the next chord. He used only down strokes, never down then up.

Recall from Chapter 8 that the third and seventh are the most important tones in a dominant 7 chord. Now consider this coincidence: The third and seventh of every dominant 7 chord are the seventh and third of the chord that is the tritone substitution (Chapter 16) of the first chord. For example.

The third and seventh of C7 are E and B♭.

The tritone substitution (flatted fifth) of C7 is G♭7.

The third and seventh of G♭7 are B♭ and E.

Consequently, if the chord chart calls for a C7, you might play this combination of notes on the guitar.

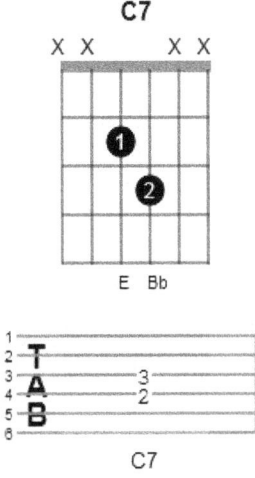

Furthermore, if the chord chart calls for G♭7 (or F#7: same thing), you can play the same chord you played for C7.

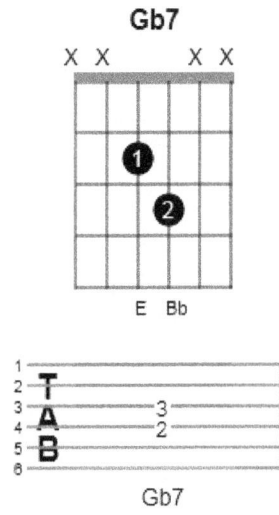

The only difference between the two grids and tabs are the chord symbols. The bass player will handle the root and define the harmonic context into which your chord fits.

The form can move up and down the fretboard to change chords, of course, but it is also transposable from side to side. Freddie did not usually use forms that employed strings 5 and 6 because they tend to sound muddy due to the lower tones. Likewise, he kept out of the upper register mostly playing strings 4, 3, and sometimes 2. You might experiment to find the forms that you prefer to hear.

There are twelve possible root notes, so there are only six forms that you'll need to play the twelve dominant 7 chords. Here they are:

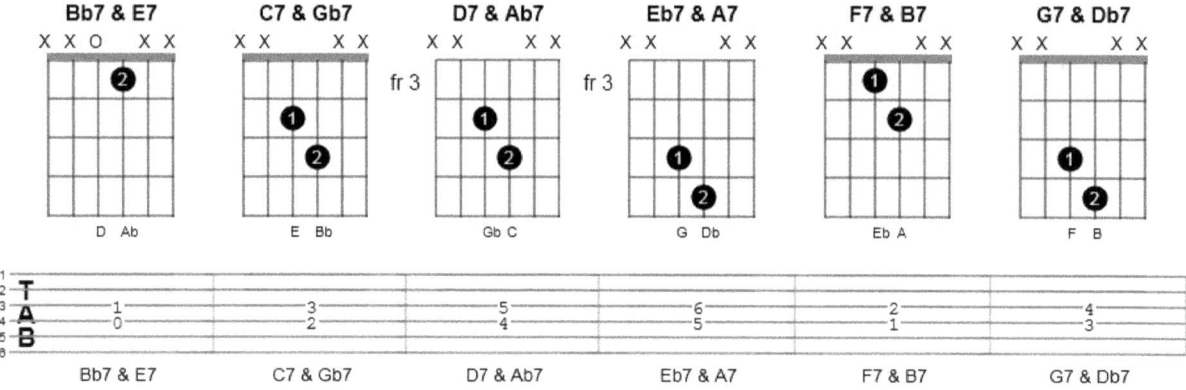

These are the chord grids closest to the nut. There are many more than these, of course, because you have the entire fretboard to move around on, using these and other forms, and the one you choose will depend on where your hand happens to be positioned when the next chord comes up.

It is important to note that Freddie was strumming these chords. Consequently, he had to mute the unplayed strings in each chord, which he did with fingers not in use. That was the effect he wanted, to use muted strings to emulate the drums. Often it looked like he was fingering the complete chord but all but the two or three notes he wanted to play were muted with the other fingers. It will take practice to figure out exactly how you want to finger some strings and mute others in all the chord forms and positions.

Freddie's guitar strings were set higher than most players prefer. It takes strong chops to press high strings to make good contact with the frets. But because his style involved muting most of the strings while he played only two or three of them, the high strings facilitated this muting. The closer a string is to the fret, the more likely it is to touch the fret and sound the note when you touch it. With Freddie's guitar, that was not a problem.

Now let's put Freddie's method to use. Remember the basic twelve-bar blues progression from Chapter 13. Here is its chord sheet again.

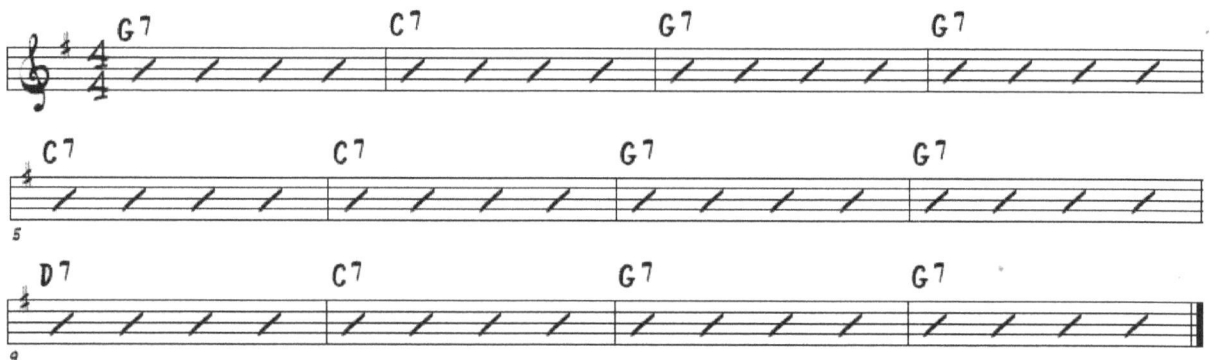

The three chords can be played Freddie-style with the simple application of these three grids:

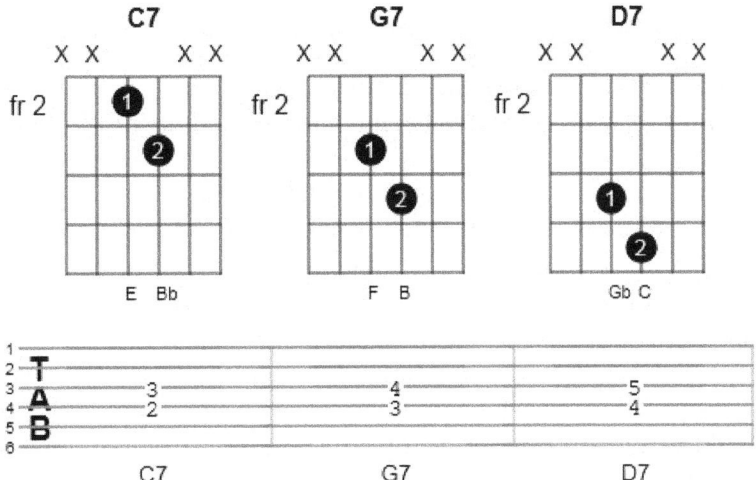

Exercise: Play the *Blues in G* backing track and practice Freddie's chord forms.

If you haven't guessed it by now, here's a bit of a surprise. Those same three grids can be used to play the blues in D♭, too. Why? Because the G7 chord and the D♭7 chord are one another's tritone substitution and use compatible grids as do the C7 chord and the G♭7 chord and the D7 chord and the A♭7 chord.

Exercise: Adjust the backing track player to other key signatures and practice Freddie's chord forms in those keys.

There is, of course, a lot more to know. Besides dominant 7s, you need groups of two and three notes to fit major chords, minor chords, diminished chords, augmented chords, and so on. Search the Internet for transcriptions of Freddie's accompaniments.

Chapter 21. Comping

Depending on who you talk to, *comping* means different things. For our purposes, comping, which is a short way of saying "accompanying," refers to the playing of chords not in strict time with the rhythm, that is, not a hard four-beat strumming, such as you've been learning up to now in this book.

Comping, for our discussion, is the playing of chords on and off the beat in a manner that states the harmonic context without playing a chord on every beat or maintaining a solid beat. It's what a piano player does during an instrumental solo or ensemble. It's what the guitar player can do when there's no piano player or when you and the piano player take turns comping. If you both comp at the same time, it's unlikely that you will be comping compatible rhythmic patterns. Typically one of you lays out while the other comps.

The first thing you should do when you begin to study comping is to listen to other guitar players doing it. They might play only one or two chords each measure. They play ahead of and after the beat. They sustain chords or play them *staccato*. Generally they make it up as they go, playing the correct chords but playing them when they want to, when to their ears it sounds best, a way to complement the soloist's lines and not get in the way.

You'll probably find that players have acquired a vocabulary of rhythmic patterns that they use. The patterns aren't dependent on the chords, only on the rhythmic nature of the accompaniment. The idea is to put the chords under the soloist or vocalist and to not interfere. Their solo is the feature. Your job is to pay attention to the solo and insert chords to make the solo sound good.

If there's a piano player, don't comp with him. Either lay out or play rhythm guitar in time and stay in the background.

To comp effectively, you must listen to the lines the soloist plays or the vocalist sings. You should know the tune's melody and its lyrics too if there are any. Then you comp chords at places where the featured performance is quiet.

Of course, in a be-bop or scat solo, it's impossible to predict the next line, which means you have to listen. If you are familiar with the player, if you have worked with that player many times, it's easier. Otherwise, you need to know what the traditional improvisational idioms are in order to find you way through the choruses without playing intrusive accompaniments.

Here are two choruses of Blues in G with some alternate changes in rhythmic notation to show how you might comp for twenty-four measures.

Exercise: Play the *Blues in G* backing track and practice these rhythmic patterns.

Notice the rests, particularly the full-measure rests at measures 3, 13, and 15. These illustrate how you leave room for the soloist and that accompaniment doesn't have to fill every measure.

> *I was playing in the Harry James ghost band under the leadership of the late, great trumpet player Art Depew. It was our first rehearsal and I was playing a lot of accompaniment. Art stopped the tune and said, "Less is more, Al. Just keep time" I got the message.*

I won't take comping any further than this. It should demonstrate how the idiom works. After studying and playing this, you should practice such patterns, make up more, and fly by the seat of your pants.

Chapter 22. Improvisation

Improvisation is the art of devising and playing extemporaneous melodies on the fly, melodies that match the harmonic context of the tune being played.

Improvisation is essential to jazz, but jazz isn't the only kind of music in which musicians improvise. Players of bluegrass, rock, lounge music, show tunes, chamber music, and all forms of pop music often employ degrees of improvisation in their performances.

This book does not teach improvisation. You can buy books that say they do, but I don't believe improvisation can be effectively taught with words. I'm not sure it can be taught with anything. It can be *learned* but it can't be taught, at least not by me. A teacher can expose you to the components of improvisation, some of which are described in this chapter, others of which are based in musical theory (Chapter 8). After that, you're on your own.

The best way, in this writer's opinion, to learn improvisation is to first, listen to those players whose improvisational skills you admire, and then try to play like them.

Some musicians have a natural aptitude for improvisation. They learn and improvise well-formed and pleasing lines much more quickly than some of their peers.

Some gravitate naturally to it without ever learning the formal terms and structure of music theory. Others never quite get the hang of it no matter how much they study. They learn the mechanics of improvisational theory—scales, arpeggios, licks, and so on—but they never figure out how to apply that knowledge to their impromptu solos.

An improvisation must respect the rhythmic jazz feel of the tune being played. There are players who understand the concepts, the theory, and can play their instruments, but their time is not precise. They play what is called a "wiffle-waffle" style of improvisation. You have to nail the time. Hit the beats and the off-beats. Kick some butt. Don't be tentative or bashful. Play those lines.

That might lead you to conclude that you need a special gift and that without it, you'll never get past the most elementary levels of improvisation. Maybe so, maybe not. But gifted or not, you won't learn it without working for it. There is no silver bullet. It takes time, dedication and practice.

You might also conclude that you don't need formal musical training. That's possible. Many gifted jazz musicians can't read a note of music and/or wouldn't know a C7 from a Gdim. It is my belief, however, that if those players would augment their natural talents with some formal education, their abilities, and consequently, their talent could escalate to heights beyond even their own expectations.

So, what exactly is improvisation?

Improvisation in jazz and other music genres can be described as spontaneous composition of melody lines based on known changes in a chosen style of playing.

That said, how do you compose in real time? It begins, of course, with knowing the tune. If you don't know the tune, or at least the chord changes, you probably can't improvise a new melody that fits. There are exceptions to this. Experienced horn players can hear the tune's chord changes as they are played by the pianist or guitar player and lay down lines of new melody against the changes they hear. You are probably not there yet. And, of course, if you are told that the tune employs the changes of another tune you know, you can improvise on those changes without ever having heard the tune you're playing.

Listen to the Improvisers

Pick a tune that you know and listen to other players improvise on it. If you listen to Pat Martino or Joe Pass you might be discouraged. Those guys are monsters. But don't try to be them. Just hear what they are doing and take from that what you can. The main thing you gain from lots of listening is your understanding of how good improvisation sounds.

Try to Improvise

Start up your backing track of the tune you were listening to (Chapter 23) and try to play lines of improvised melody against the chord changes. Many jazz students begin with the blues (Chapter 13) and I suggest you do the same.

Lines in this context are melodic passages that comprise one note at a time. The melody line. Play only one note at a time as you improvise. There will be time enough later to learn to play lines and chords along with them. For now, keep it as simple as possible. And listen to the pros. Most guitar improvisations, especially when there are other players in the rhythm section, employ one note lines much as a trumpet or sax player would do.

Play simple lines that include the chords' root notes and fifths. Just that. Get used to what they sound like. Add the thirds. Later you can fill in the other notes to form lines.

Play the blues in G. Use a tempo with which you are comfortable. If 120 bpm is too fast, try 60. If that's too easy, try 90. And so on. For each measure, play a simple line that fits.

What fits? First, remember our number one rule.

If it sounds right, it's right.

All you have to do is play something that sounds right.

Yeah, I know, that's not a lot of help. So what can you improvise that you can be sure will sound right? What notes? What phrases?

Remember, listen to experienced players. Don't always try to copy them note for note. Try instead to be influenced by what they play.

Hum Your Improvisation

Try humming an improvised line against the chord changes. Don't worry about what notes you're humming other than that they fit the chords. Hum out loud what you hear in your mind. If you can hear it, you can hum it. Eventually, if you can hum it, you can play it.

Do this in small passages, only a few measures at a time. If you don't like what you hummed, hum something else. When you like what you hummed, try to pick the notes on the guitar. When you can play that line, hum something that fits the next several measures and learn to play that passage.

Now, how do you relate what you've heard, hummed, and played to the changes themselves? All you know is that the notes fit the chord changes, which means they sound right.

Match Notes and Chords

Determine the tonal center (Chapter 10) of the passage you are learning. If you're in a major key center, play notes from the major scale of that key. Not necessarily the scale itself, but notes chosen from that scale. Those will fit. Play those notes. Between beats, play what we call *passing tones*, notes that aren't in the scale but that pass chromatically from one scale note to another.

Playing Outside

Playing lines and going *outside* was popularized in the early 1960s by the new forms of modern jazz being played by Miles Davis, Bill Evans, and John Coltrane. It didn't start then and with those players. Art Tatum was going outside on the piano in the 1930s. Not many players tried to copy his style though, because his playing was way beyond anything they'd ever heard.

The outside idiom involves improvising lines based on the so-called *altered* scale of the current tonal center.

The altered scale of a dominant 7 chord is a seven-tone scale that contains the chord's root, 3rd and 7th notes. All the other notes are altered. For example, the C7 altered scale is:

C, D♭, E♭, E, F#, A♭, B♭.

Players go *outside* by playing lines based on this scale when the rest of the band is playing a C7 chord. The practice usually stays outside briefly and comes back inside shortly thereafter.

There is a way to go outside without trying to remember what's altered and what is not. Move the first note in the scale to the end and you have the D♭ harmonic minor scale shown here:

D♭, E♭, E, F#, A♭, B♭. C

To sound like you're playing outside, play a line a half-tone up from where you'd play it against the current dominant 7 chord. The E might become an F when you do that, but who cares? It's outside.

Blue Notes

There are many musical occasions other than playing outside when you can play notes not included in the tonal center's major scale, notes that are not passing tones. The notes you can play are called *blue notes*.

A blue note is a flatted third, fifth, or seventh played in the context of the current tonal center. They're called blue notes because they fit especially well when you're playing the blues. They have a sad sound to them even in an up-tempo tune. They are like morphing into a sad minor key within the framework of a major key.

Lead guitar players love to bend blue notes, sustaining them for maximum effect. Listen to any B.B. King solo for an example.

Flatted 3rd

The most recognizable blue note is the flatted third. Against a G chord, B♭ is that blue note. You would think the underlying chord would be G minor when the (improvised) melody note is a B♭ but it typically is not. The blue note in this context is similar to a raised 9th chord (Chapter 7), but it works with major chords as well as dominant 7 chords.

So the B♭ blue note can occur in a G major chord, a G7, a G7(♭9) and a G7(#9).

Flatted 5th

A flatted fifth is a form of bluesy dissonance when played against a major or dominant 7 chord, not to be confused with a tritone substitution (Chapter 16). The be-boppers discovered it as they searched for alternative and hip ways to improvise that didn't sound like traditional jazz and swing.

It became common for players to end a tune by playing the tonic's flatted fifth where the root note of the tonic was expected.

Eddie Condon, famous Dixieland guitar player, humorist, and bandleader, once said about be-bop jazz musicians, "They flat their fifths. We drink ours."

Arpeggios and Scales

An arpeggio is playing the notes in a chord up and down. Look at any grid with any form in it. Play the notes one by one, ascending up the chord. Then play them again, descending top to bottom. That's an arpeggio. Actually, it's two arpeggios.

You learned about scales in Chapter 8. You can run a scale from its lowest to highest note through two octaves without moving your left hand to another position. This fretboard picture shows you how.

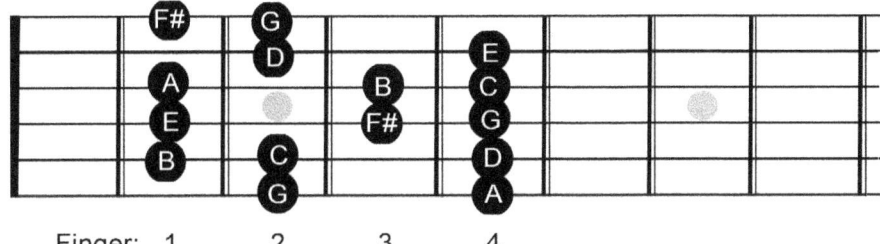

Exercise: With your left hand in the second position play the G major scale as shown above. Start on string 6 and pick notes on frets left to right as shown in the diagram. Move up one string and continue, picking and moving until you've played two octaves of the G scale.

Exercise: Reverse the order and play the scale from the top note to the bottom.

Exercise: Move your hand to the third position (up one fret) and repeat the scale, although now you're playing two octaves of the A♭ major scale. And so on.

Knowing the tonal center (Chapter 10) of the current passage and how to arpeggiate and run scales are tools to use in making improvisations. They also help your ear know what note to play and where it is when your imagination dreams up a new line for your improvisation.

Conventional wisdom advises you to "arpeggiate up, scale down" when improvising. Give it a try.

Licks

Licks are canned phrases that musicians use where the phrases fit. They can be as simple as a triplet and as complex as a series of jumps all over the fretboard.

All licks have this one thing in common: you've heard them before, perhaps not in the same place in the same tune or with the same tonal center, but jazz musicians have heard them and recognize them.

Some licks are closely associated with well-known players, and if you use them, your fellow musicians on the bandstand will acknowledge your choice as being the "Parker" lick, or the "Montgomery" lick. Others are generic and everyone uses them. An example is the "Woody Woodpecker" lick, which contains a triplet arpeggio on the first beat of the lick and a pair of closing notes on the next beat. It got its name because the lick resembles the signature call that the cartoon character uses. D*ubada da-da*! It usually has a lead-in note to introduce the lick.

A common lick is the grace note. *Da-dum.* Some players use them everywhere, prefixing the first note of every phrase with a grace note, especially in ballads. Trumpet players love grace notes. They're easy to finger and lip.

There are hundreds of licks, and hundreds of ways to use them. Listen for them in your jazz recording collection. When you hear what you think is a lick, write it down or pick it out on your guitar. Then try it in different tonal centers.

A good way to improve your jazz lick vocabulary is from a book that teaches licks, and many such books are available for the guitar. With a few licks under your belt, you are ready to amaze your pals at the next jam session.

It has been said that what separates a great jazz musician from an average one is how many licks each knows and how well they know to apply them in improvisations. A great player can play a concert without repeating a lick. But they're in the music nonetheless. Listen for them. Copy them. Add them to your jazz vocabulary.

Quotes

A popular form of lick is the *quote* wherein a musician inserts the notes of a passage from a different tune into what's being played at the time. Some quotes become clichés. Players quote the *Star Trek* theme in the first four bars of *Out of Nowhere* so often that it has become a standard part of any improvised solo on that tune. And they'll revel in their cleverness every time too, looking around to make sure everyone got it. Another worn out cliché is the refrain of *The Christmas Song* ("Chestnuts roasting...") inserted in place of the bridge for *Body and Soul*.

Some jazz musicians are eloquent with their quotes, inserting them where you'd least expect them. Others rely on the clichés or don't play quotes at all.

> *A band I played in for several years had a ritual for whenever anyone played a quote. They'd all pantomime pulling a chit from their pockets and writing it out. The chit was so you'd know you had to buy drinks for the band as penance for the quote.*

My friend and roommate on the road, the late Lou Mauro, a great bass player, used to complain that if he came up with a clever quote on the spot, all the players would be using it the following night. Of course, Lou complained about everything, but that's another story.

> *One night I quoted* Moon Over Miami *at the first four bars of* Perdido. *When it got around to the tenor player, he copied my quote. I told Lou about it later. He said, "Some guys can't even wait a day."*

Quotes can derail a tune.

> *I quoted Ja-Da as the intro to* Georgia on my Mind. *Or maybe it was the other way around. Half the band began playing one tune, the rest of the band was playing the other. The inevitable train wreck ensued. Wild Bill Davison, the leader, shook his finger at me when the tune was over and said, "Now that was your fault." He was right.*

Quotes are anathema to some musicians. If that musician happens to be the leader, quotes can get you in trouble.

> *The leader of a successful Dixieland band—some will guess the band right off; there aren't that many successful Dixieland bands—whose roots are planted firmly in traditional jazz, enforces an ironclad rule: no quotes. I asked one of his musicians whether everyone respects that rule to the letter. "Naw," he said. "We just quote tunes he wouldn't know."*

Impromptu Composition

This is the purest form of improvisation. You aren't thinking about chord changes or applying scales, arpeggios, licks or quotes. You are composing a fresh melody as you play. You hear the next note and you play it without consideration of where it fits in the harmonic context. You just know that it will sound okay.

There's not much more I can say about that. Your skills as an impromptu composer grow with experience and practice.

Transcriptions

A *transcription* is an improvised solo that someone has put to paper so others can play it. I spent a lot of my childhood transcribing jazz solos from records. Then I'd memorize the solos. I still play some of them today just for the heck of it. They are great solos.

You don't have to laboriously write down transcriptions today. You can buy books of transcribed solos of your favorite jazz players. Many transcriptions are available online.

How do transcriptions help you learn to improvise? If you just use them as exercises in music reading and memorization, they don't necessarily instill in you the thought processes that the soloists used to come up with those solos.

You can eventually play a great player's solos note for note. But why do that? It's already been done. Be original when you perform.

That said, if you play transcriptions and think about the chord changes, you might get inside the head of the soloist. For this chord or change, this is what the soloist thinks, and so on. Then rather than trying to play exactly like that soloist, you should be influenced by him along with the influences of the other soloists you've transcribed and copied. Those influences, combined with what you bring to the exercises from your own imagination, will help you form your own voice.

Reward and Punishment

Every time you play a line that pleases you, that pleasure is a *reward*. Conversely, every time you play a line that displeases you, the displeasure is a *punishment*. These are the basic tenets of so-called *behavior modification*. Rewards are positive reinforcement of appropriate behavior. Punishment is negative reinforcement of inappropriate behavior. And by repeating the appropriate behavior and receiving the reward, you condition yourself to behave appropriately, thus learning to play good lines as a matter of habit.

Others can contribute to your rewards and punishment, and they can often do more harm than good. For example, you'll often hear musicians congratulate one another on their improvisations by saying things such as, "I hear you talkin', man." And they do it even when the chorus sucked. That's positive reinforcement of inappropriate behavior, it makes the player think he's doing okay, and he never improves. Maybe he'd never improve anyway, but unless his friends stop lauding his playing, he never *can* improve. If you don't want to give negative reinforcement to keep from hurting his feelings, at least withhold the positive vibes. Behavior ignored often becomes behavior abandoned.

If you don't like a line you've played, don't play it again just because you can. Just don't play it again. Repeat the lines you like. As you pile up the self-inflicted positive reinforcements, your behavior is subconsciously modified to be appropriate—to play good lines.

Chapter 23. Practicing

Face it. You have to practice. Your goal should be to make practicing enjoyable so that you'll be eager to escape to the practice room and get to it. Some of it will be repetitious and tedious and some of it will be fun. Work and play.

> *A musician on his first trip to NYC stops another musician on the street and asks, "How do you get to Carnegie Hall?"*
>
> *The other musician answers, "Practice, man, practice."*

That might be the oldest musician's joke known to the profession—its origins have never been established—but there is truth in the punch line. To be a proficient and successful musician, you must practice.

> *Concert pianist Vladimir Horowitz once said, "When I don't practice for a day, I notice. When I don't practice for two days, the orchestra notices. When I don't practice for three days, the audience notices."*

There are as many approaches to a student's practice regimen as there are guitar teachers, it would seem. If you have a teacher, by all means practice what he or she prescribes. But to get the most out of the lessons in this book, the best practice discipline in my opinion is this:

Play tunes

This should be obvious. Practice what you want to play, the tunes you like in the styles you want to learn. You can set aside time for scales and arpeggios, but they alone are not what you'll be playing when you perform. They help build your chops but they don't teach you tunes.

Here are more guidelines in no particular order for you to develop effective practicing habits:

Tune up

Keep your guitar in tune (Chapter 3). Learning to play properly and by ear is far easier when the instrument is playing well too.

Play in time

It's not enough to play the right chords. You have to play the right tempo too. Every tune starts with a count-off. *One, two, one, two, three, four.*

Stick with the original tempo—the one you or the leader set up when you started playing the tune—and do not pause to find your way to a missed chord. Keep playing the tune and catch up where you can. You can return later to the troublesome passage and iron out the problem.

Remember, on the stand the band won't wait for you to find that elusive chord. A productive practice session teaches you not only the tune and its chords but how to play with discipline on the stand in front of an audience.

Unless you get hopelessly lost in a tune, keep playing even if you lose your place, don't know the next chord, know it but don't know how to form it, and so on. Your job as rhythm guitar player is to play the chords and keep time. Keeping time is the more important of those duties, so when you're lost, keep strumming. Let your left hand fingers mute the strings so that they don't sound their notes, but they sound time beats. When you find your place again, resume playing chords. Chances are nobody will notice during a performance, and your practice sessions should simulate the bandstand as much as possible. The main objective is, keep the tune going. The show must go on, train wrecks notwithstanding.

Playing in time also means maintaining a steady tempo. Do not rush or drag. If the drummer, bass player, or both are rushing or dragging, there's not a lot you can do other than complain. Time is everyone's responsibility. Some bass players play on top of the beat, which means they play their notes a fraction of a second before the beat. Don't chase them. Don't try to get on top with them. They'll adjust to get on top of your beat, and the tempo will be steadily rushed.

> **Exercise:** Select a tune that you know well, one with a medium tempo. Turn your recorder on. Kick off the tune but don't use a metronome or backing track. When you reach the end of the tune. listen to the beginning of the recorded tune and then move to the end. Are the tempos at either end of the tune consistent? If not, you need to keep working on time.

Repeat the exercise at various tempos.

What can you do if you're rushing or dragging the tempo? Try this:

> **Exercise:** Start your metronome at the troublesome tempo. Use a metronome that ticks audibly. You don't want beeps, you want ticks. Don't watch the metronome's pendulum if it has one. Now, clap along with the metronome. Try to clap such that your clapping drowns out the metronome's clicks. Every time you hear a click, your time is off.

Do this exercise many times at different tempos. Remember, you are a part of a *rhythm* section. Maybe you *are* the rhythm section. The band, the dancers, the audience, and whoever pays your wages depend on you to maintain a steady beat.

Work on it.

Learn the lyrics

If the tunes have lyrics, if they are *songs* in the literal definition of the word, learn the lyrics. Allow them to run in the back of your mind while you play the tunes. I know, you're concentrating on changes and tonal centers at the same time, but the lyrics are a large part of the original musical composition, and if you know them, they will influence the lines that you improvise. If your listeners, even the ones with no formal musical education, can hear the song they know within the framework of your improvisation, you're doing it right. But if you can't hear it, they probably won't either. Thinking the lyrics while you play a song also helps you keep your place in the tune.

When you're not practicing, sing—in the shower, as you drive, wherever you can sound out without embarrassing yourself. Sing, sing, sing.

> *I was once driving through town with the windows open and singing* The Man I Love. *I got a lot of stares from other drivers and pedestrians. Be careful about where and what you sing.*

Use backing tracks

I find it most helpful to practice with backing tracks playing the tunes I want to play. And the best tool for that is a program called *Band-in-a-Box* (They call it BIAB for short.) With that program and the countless tune files you can download, you can practice almost any tune at any tempo in any key and in any style.

BIAB generates realistic backgrounds by using loops recorded by human musicians as opposed to synthesized sequences.

The program itself doesn't come with many tunes, but you can find them on the Internet and ones that go with these lessons on my website at http://www.alstevens.com/jazzguitar.

BIAB has an ancient user interface that takes some getting used to. But once you've got it mastered, it does everything you'd want a musical learning tool to do.

If you have your own compositions that you want to practice, BIAB lets you program the melody, chord changes, style, tempo, key, and all kinds of playback-related parameters such as the number of choruses to play, repeats, endings, and so on.

If the downloaded tune file uses conventional chord changes, you can reprogram it to use the hip substitutions you've learned here and will learn from other musicians.

> *Disclaimer: I have no financial interest in the BIAB product. The company that owns and distributes it is unaware of this endorsement.*

As far as I know, BIAB is the only program on the market that accomplishes all that a practicing musician needs in the way of accompaniment.

Practice what you already know

We often hear that practicing what we've already learned won't help us advance. I disagree. In other disciplines it's called "review." In medical and legal professions, it's called "practicing" even when it's being done for clients as part of the profession.

Practicing what you already know serves two purposes. First, it gives you the confidence and positive feedback you get when you play something properly. Second, it reinforces earlier lessons and helps you retain and not forget them. So, take a break from the hard lessons at hand and play a tune or exercise you already know. You'll enjoy doing that, and, after all, learning is a lot easier when you have a good time doing it.

Practice two-chord changes

Pick a dominant 7th and a tonic, G7 and Cmaj7, for example, and practice that change repetitively. Try four beats per chord. Tap your foot with the rhythm. Go slow at first. Then as you become more accurate with the forms, speed up. The idea is to get those forms into your muscle memory so that you don't have to think about them when they come up in a tune. Speak the chord symbol names as you play to get them into your subconscious memory too so you can associate each chord with its symbol, its sound, and its feel on the fretboard.

> *A musician's joke tells of when a fan requests* When Sonny Gets Blue. *The band singer doesn't know the tune. The guitar player says, "I can sing it." So they kick it off. His vocal starts out like this:*
>
> "When Sonny Gets Blue, B Flat minor seven..."

After you learn the first two-chord sequence, move your hand up a position, which in this case would be A♭7 and D♭maj7, and repeat the exercise. Each day, practice the new position. Then finish off by practicing the change up and down the fretboard. Say the chord symbols when you play them.

Do not keep grids or tabs of these chords in front of you while you practice. All that does it make you dependent on the grids. You want to learn what the music sounds and feels like, not what it looks like.

With the two-chord changes under your belt, add the two-minor-seven chord at the front and practice those ii-V-I three-chord changes up and down the fretboard (Chapter 11).

Throughout your practice sessions, remember that you have at least three forms with which to play each chord depending on which string gets the root. Practice the variations until the changes become second nature.

Look at the charts

Don't look at the fretboard all the time. When you are reading charts with a band, you need to keep your eye on the chart so you know the changes you are expected to play, the navigation of the chart, and so that you don't get lost in the arrangement.

Look away from the charts

This teaches you to play tunes without relying on the charts. It's also necessary if you are accompanying yourself on vocals to be able to play while you sing and pay attention to the audience. Again, don't look at the fretboard any more than is absolutely necessary.

Read ahead

When reading charts, whether they be lead sheets, chord charts, or big band charts, whether they be in slash, rhythmic, standard notation, or some combination (Chapter 5), it's important that you read ahead of yourself. This comes with practice, but if you don't practice doing exactly this, it will never come.

Begin by looking at the first measure. Remember, unless you are soloing, you are interested only in the chords and the rhythmic patterns if any are given. Put the first measure to memory. Then, as you play the first measure from memory, read and put to memory the second measure. Read ahead like that for the entire chart.

It's not easy at first. It takes a bit of a split personality. Your conscious mind concentrates on the next measure while your subconscious mind plays the current one.

Being able to do this is the first step to learning to *sight read*, to read a chart at near performance levels the first time you see it. It's an ability you'll need in order to play in a big band.

When you can comfortably read charts by looking a measure ahead, expand your scan to two measures ahead, which you assimilate while you are playing the current two.

It is helpful to realize that eventually, each measure you look at will often be a chordal and rhythmic pattern you've seen countless times before. You'll see a sequence of the I-vi-ii-V changes, for example, and know immediately how to play all four chords and how to move from one to the other. Naturally, that takes experience and practice.

When you are able to read ahead two measures at a time, expand your scan to four.

Time will come when you look at a many-measure passage or even a whole chart beginning to end and realize that you already know the complete set of chord changes in the key being shown. You'll say, "aha, rhythm changes," or "eureka, Sears Roebuck bridge," or "got it, blues changes," and so on.

The only way to get there, though, is with practice. Lots of it.

Learn each tune in several keys

Use your backing track software to change the key several times of each tune that you learn. Become familiar with the usual keys for jazz music, which unlike rock and country does not stick to open-string keys and chords. The usual jazz keys are C, E♭, F, G, A♭, and B♭, with an occasional departure into D♭. Few jazz tunes are in the keys that country players are used to, A, D, E, and G and less often, B. One prominent jazz tune in D is the bossa nova, *Wave*. Learn that tune in D and you can mostly ignore the key for all the other tunes. Sometimes singers will request an unfamiliar key. You can usually slide them up or down a half-tone to put the tune where it will be comfortable for the rest of the band.

Listen to other guitar players

This is important. Devote a good portion of your study to the works of others, the players you'd like to emulate. Listen to how they thread their playing through the changes and substitutions. Call their performances up on YouTube and watch them play. Observe how they hold the instrument and what both hands are doing. Make note of the tunes they play that you like and add those tunes to your list of tunes to learn.

Have a place to practice

It's best to have a quiet, isolated practice room, preferably one in which you won't be interrupted and your practice won't interfere with the lives of others. Everybody's situation is different so I'll leave it to you to set yourself up with a workable studio.

Use comfortable tempos

Set the playback of the backing track for a tune to a tempo with which you can keep up. As you get comfortable with the slower tempo, speed it up. Do that until you're playing the tune at performance tempos.

Repeat difficult passages

If you run across a difficult passage that needs attention, use the backing track software to loop it so you can concentrate on problem spots until the problems go away.

Keep your interest alive

If you get bored with a tune, set it aside and practice another one. Nothing discourages the learning of an intricate art form like tedium. It's why so many players object to practicing scales.

Practice a lot

I won't try to tell you how many hours a day you should practice. That's up to you. Not everybody has all the time in the world. Most people—even guitar players—have lives. Some teachers recommend practice sessions of no more than fifteen minutes. If that works for you, fine. But bear in mind the 10,000 hour rule, which maintains that it takes 10,000 hours of deliberate practice to become a world-class practitioner in any field. Be grateful that playing the guitar is a labor of love. Practicing might become tedious, though, so use your practice time wisely to achieve an even balance of skill-building and enjoyment.

Don't overdo it

If your fingertips, hand or arm joints or muscles hurt, give it a rest. Take your hands off the guitar and flex them. Pushing an injured or strained appendage past its limits can do serious damage and end your playing career. If you're tired, get some sleep. Eat properly. Drink lots of water. Don't smoke, even when you're not practicing. Leave the recreational drugs out of your practice regimen. They'll just make you think you're playing better than you are.

Involve other musicians

This is an important aspect to productive practicing. Whenever possible, get together with other players to "shed" your music. Whether you congregate in a garage, busk on the street for tips, or attend public jam sessions, make sure you include other musicians as part of your learning process. You'll learn faster if the other musicians are better than you. Lots better. You rise to the challenge, and more experienced players can and will mentor you and show you the ropes.

Appendix A: Chords

This appendix contains the chords you've learned in a summary organization. A guitarist can play many more chords than the ones this appendix shows. This is your reference to the forms of chords that will get you through most gigs. If you don't know how to form a particular chord, look here.

Using this Appendix

The grids and tabs in this appendix present *transposable* chord forms (Chapter 6) for the chords closest to the guitar's nut. It is not necessary to show the chords for all the possible root notes. Just move your hand up some number of positions to get to the root and, therefore, the chord you want to play. See *Finding the Root Notes* in Chapter 4.

The grids present the chords for forms that use root notes on strings 6, 5 and 4 and use the easiest forms to make, avoiding wide left hand stretches. Sometimes the chord itself is different from the category under which it is listed here. For example, we might use a 9 chord where a 7 is called for because first, it sounds better (Chapter 9) and second, it's an easier form to play.

There are 45 chord forms in this appendix. For now, that's all you need to learn. The forms are transposable up the fretboard. You shouldn't have to go very far up. You can stay in the first five hand positions and cover all the chords.

For example, if you play the Fmaj7 chord form shown below and play the same form up the fretboard, when you get to fret 5, you are at the Amaj7 chord. Return to the first hand position, switch to the B♭6 chord with its root on string 5, and you can continue upward from there. The fifth position puts you on the E6 chord, and a return to position 1, string 4 root, continues your upward travel of major chords.

> *Great country guitar player Chet Atkins once told an interviewer that he'd built an entire career recording and performing while rarely getting above the fifth hand position.*

You don't have to switch at position five though. You can stay with a form and proceed up the fretboard until the body of the guitar gets in the way. The main thing is to know where all the chords are in all their forms. Know that and you can play accompaniments to any jazz or standard tune if you have a chord chart in front of you.

Remember that my fingerings are optional and based on my hands. There are no right and wrong ways. Use fingerings that suit you, are easy to play, and are comfortable.

The Chords

Here they are, the chords you've learned in this book. Learn each form, put its name and purpose to memory, and move your left hand up and down the fretboard to find all the chords each form will play.

Major

These are vanilla transposable forms for the major chord with roots on strings 6, 5 and 4.

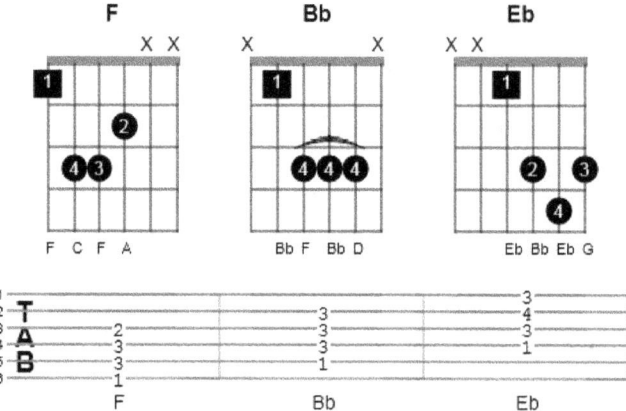

I have difficulty with the rightmost major chord form, so I usually substitute one of the following forms, which are colorful transposable forms for the major chord with roots on strings 6, 5 and 4.

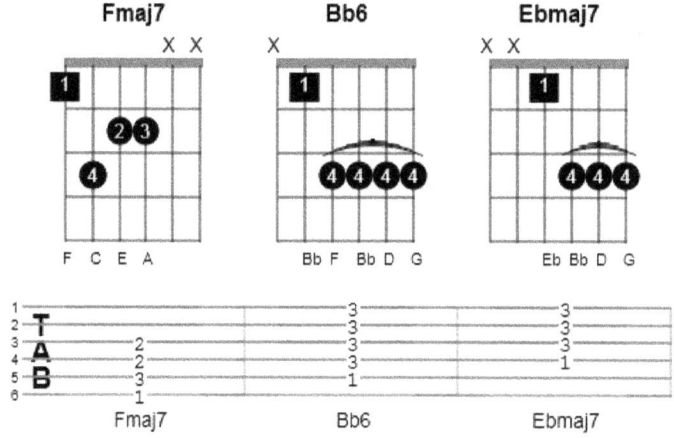

You can barre finger 1 in the Fmaj7 form all the way to string 1 to get a higher-pitched sound. The chord would look like this:

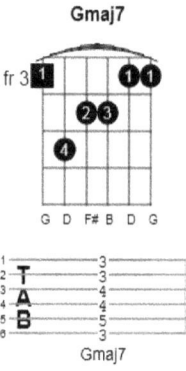

Minor

These are vanilla transposable forms for the major chord with roots on strings 6, 5 and 4.

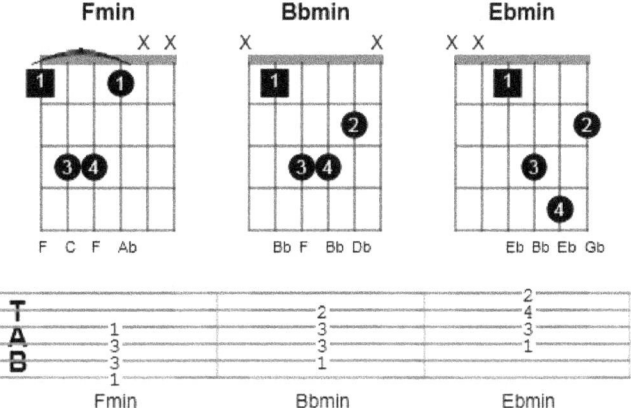

Following are more colorful minor chords. I wouldn't use the min(maj7) chord unless it was called for, usually because that major 7 note is prominent in the melody.

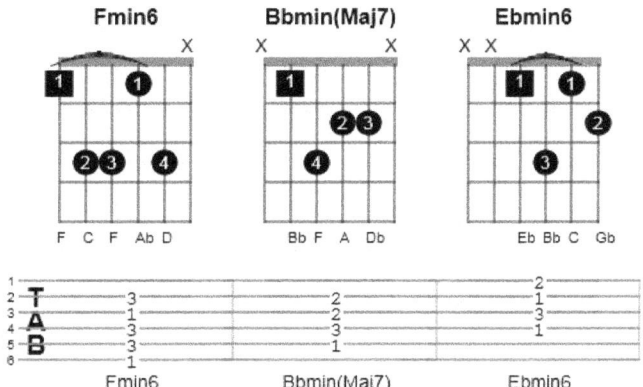

Remember from Chapter 7 that min6 chords are inversions of other min7(♭5) chords so you can substitute one for the other. For example, Fmin6 and Dmin7(♭5) are the same chord.

Dominant 7

These are vanilla transposable forms for the dominant 7 chord with roots on strings 6, 5 and 4.

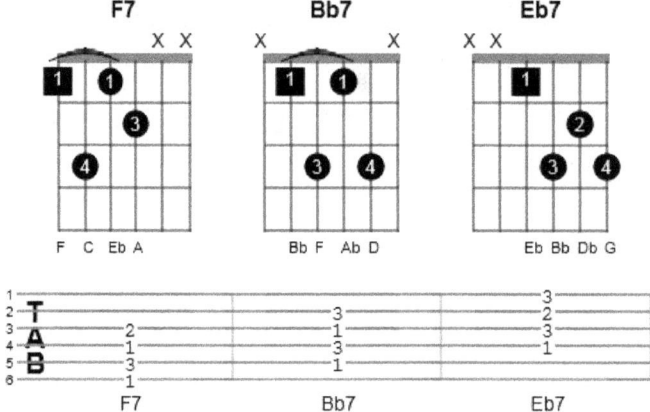

These are colorful transposable forms for the dominant 7 chord with roots on strings 6, 5 and 4.

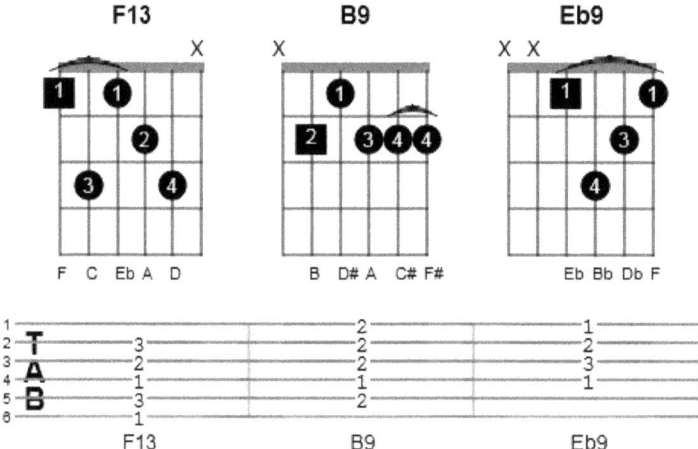

Minor 7

These are vanilla transposable forms for the minor 7 chord with roots on strings 6, 5 and 4.

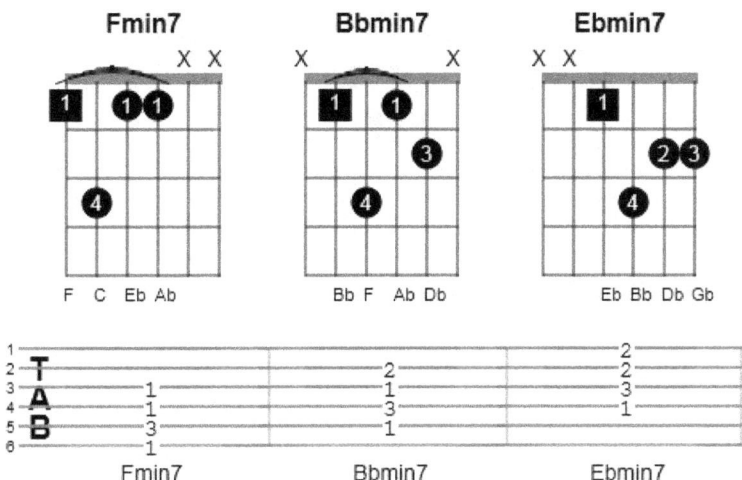

These are colorful transposable forms for the minor 7 chord with roots on strings 6 and 5.

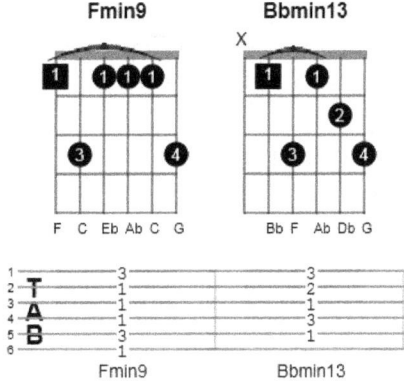

I don't have a comfortable, transposable, colorful minor 7 form with the root on string 4 that doesn't stretch my left hand beyond its natural limits, so we've provided only two forms for that chord.

Minor 7 (♭5) aka Half-diminished

These are vanilla transposable forms for the half-diminished chord with roots on strings 6, 5 and 4.

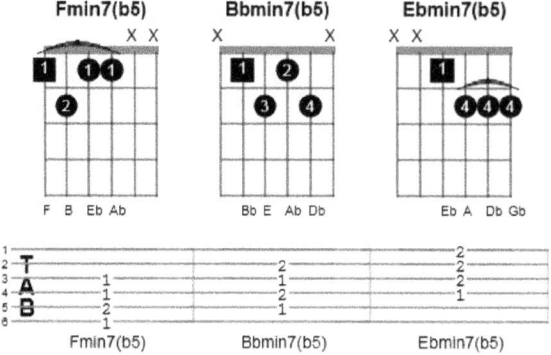

The half-diminished chord is colorful enough in its vanilla forms, so that's what's given here.

Diminished 7

These are vanilla transposable forms for the diminished 7 chord with roots on strings 6, 5 and 4.

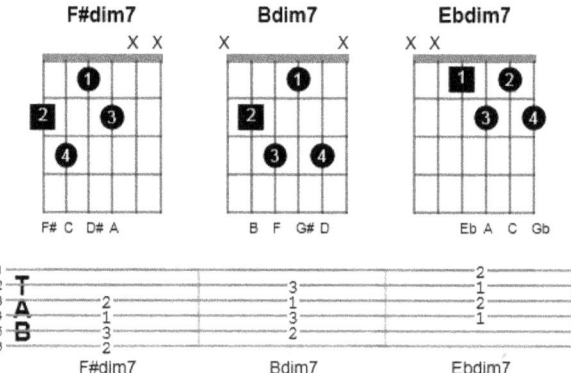

You don't need to add color tones to the diminished 7 chords. That would change them into different chords.

Dominant 7 (♭9)

Flat 9 chords have all the color they need, so we use only one form for each of the root string positions.

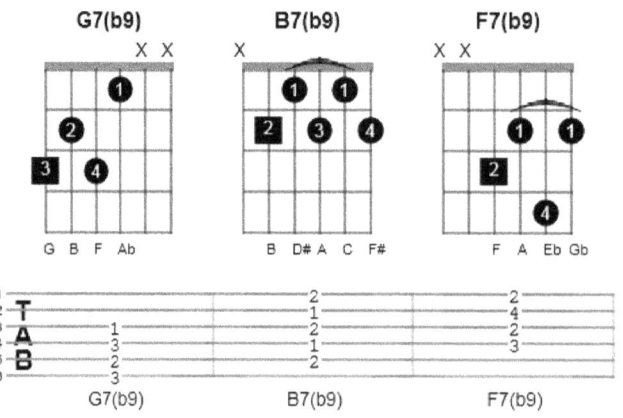

The dominant 7 chord bears a close relationship to the min7(♭5) chord of its flatted 9th as Chapter 7 explains.

Dominant 7 (♯9)

Sharp 9 chords have all the color they need, so we use only one form for each of the root string positions.

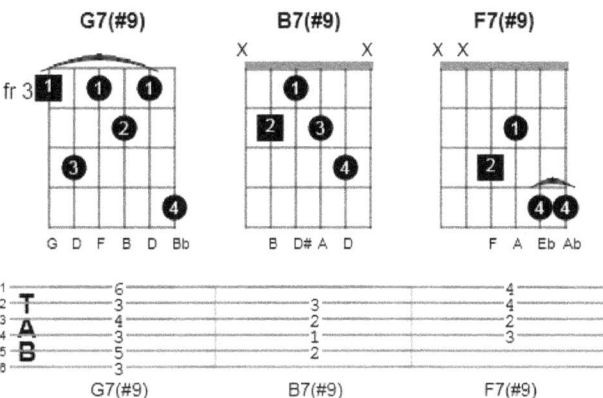

That leftmost form above is probably the stretchiest form in the book. I never play it. If it works for you, congratulations.

Augmented

Here again, we do not need colorful variations on the augmented chord. That could change its sound and its purpose in a harmonic context.

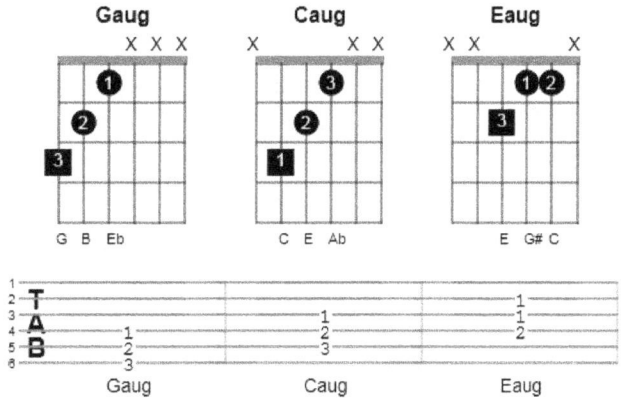

Position these three transposable forms up the fretboard up to four positions, and you have all the augmented chords covered. That's because each one is an inversion of the two augmented chords with the other two notes as roots. For example, Baug is Gaug, inversion 1 and E♭aug, inversion 2.

Augmented 7

As with others, we do not need colorful variations on the augmented 7 chord. That could change its sound and its purpose in a harmonic context.

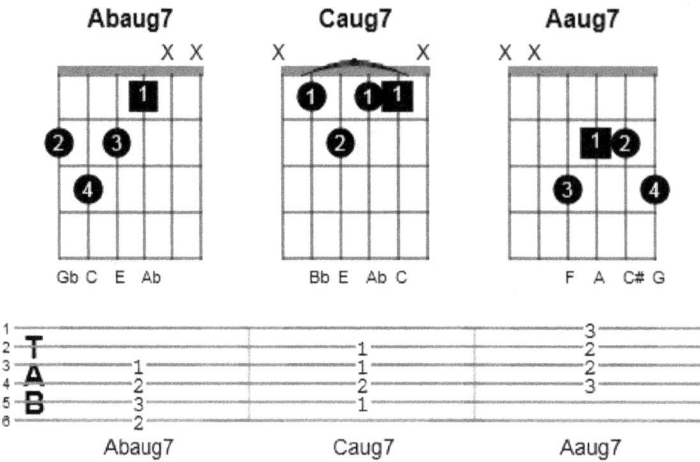

These chords are unique within these lessons in that their forms put the root on other than the lowest string played. Unlike the simple augmented chord, the augmented 7 chord does not have inversions that are other 7 augmented chords. You have to re-position your left hand to get other 7 augmented chords of the same transposable form.

Suspended

Here again, we do not need colorful variations on the suspended chord. That could change its sound and its purpose in a harmonic context.

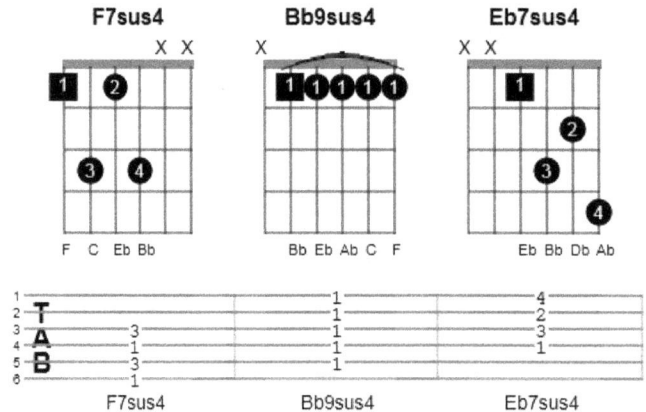

The chord symbol for suspended chords can have the 4 suffix or not. Either one is common.

That Eb7sus4 chord is a bit of a stretch for a small left hand. You might prefer to use one of the other two forms.

Summary

The chords in this appendix are ones you should know.

Bear in mind that there are many other ways to play these chords. Appendix C lists references that you can use to look up more chords and forms than you might have thought possible. This appendix is a subset of the guitar's chord vocabulary and will get you by on most jazz and commercial gigs. And it might contain all the chords you'll ever need for jazz and standard tune accompaniments.

Appendix B: Jazz Slang

These are terms and phrases you'll hear tossed about in the studio, on the bandstand, on the band bus, wherever jazz musicians hang. Some of them are affected, some are antiquated, going back sixty years or so. But here they are so you can keep up with what your peers are saying.

axe	A musician's instrument
bad	good
bandstand	the stage where you perform
beat	a measure of rhythm
blow	play jazz
bone	trombone
bop	a style of jazz developed in the 1940s
break	a pause in a tune during which one musician plays
bring us in	count off the tune's rhythm
cat	musician
change	a chord
changes	a sequence of chords
chart	an arrangement, lead sheet, or chord sheet
chick singer	female vocalist
chops	a player's endurance and stamina to play the instrument
clam	a harmonic or melodic error that stands out
combo	a small band consisting of a rhythm section and zero or more horns
comp	accompany
cool	good, pleasing
dig	like, appreciate
drag	slow down the tempo
free	a form of jazz that does not adhere to structure of any kind
front	an insert for the stand to identify the band
ghost band	name band of which the famous leader is deceased and the band continues to perform
hack meter	play too many or too few beats in a measure
head	the main refrain of the tune, the chorus
head arrangement	memorized format for the musical rendition of a tune
hip	savvy, knowledgable
house band	the band employed by the venue to accompany featured performers and those sitting in
intro	musical introduction to a tune's performance

teach yourself Rhythm Jazz Guitar, *a player's guide* – Al Stevens

jam session	gathering of musicians to play ad hoc and impromptu tunes
kack	die
kick it off	count off the tune
lay out	refrain from playing during part of a tune's performance
lick	a recognized harmonic, melodic and rhythmic pattern inserted into an improvisation
licorice stick	clarinet
mainstream	jazz based on standard popular tunes played in commercial styles
man	a name with which to address a musician
mother key	F
number	tune, so called because charts in a part's folder are numbered
obble-gobble	*obbligato*
out chorus	the last chorus of a tune's performance
outside	a style of improvisation that uses the altered scale against a dominant 7 chord
pocket	groove
play the ink	play a band chart as it was originally published and ignore manual (pencil or ink) markings
riff	an improvised ensemble pattern played behind a soloist
road map	the navigational properties of a band chart
rush	speed up the tempo
scat	improvised vocal lines with meaningless words
shed	practice a tune or a program of tunes
sit in	play as an unpaid guest with a house band
smooth jazz	a style of jazz with little or no improvisation that sounds weak and pointless to real musicians
stand	a rack for holding charts on the bandstand
swing	v. play in the pocket or groove. n. music that swings
trad	traditional jazz, usually Dixieland
train wreck	a musical mishap that ruins the tune's performance
turnaround	a passage that provides the transition between other passages
woodshed	practice

Appendix C. Resources

This appendix lists titles and links to resources available to help in your jazz guitar studies

Links

Companion site	www.alstevens.com/jazzguitar	This is where I've posted full chord charts and *Band-in-a-Box* backing tracks for the tunes we discuss in this book and many others that I like to play.
Band-in-a-Box	http://www.pgmusic.com/	You purchase the remarkable *Band-in-a-Box* program here. It is available in versions that run on Windows and Mac.
YouTube	http://www.youtube.com	Search this site for any artist and any tune to hear what the tunes sound like and who plays them and how.
Guitar Chords Chart	http://tinyurl.com/ml22phm	This is a simple website that provides grids for all the guitar chords.
Joe Pass – Solo Jazz Guitar	https://tinyurl.com/m9xfnzo	The late Joe Pass was an amazing jazz guitarist. This video is the first in a series of lessons he recorded.

Books

These are books on jazz guitar that I have used. There are many more. Search your online bookstore for these titles and for others categorized as "jazz guitar."

Swing & Big Band Guitar, Charlton Johnson

Jazz Standards for Solo Guitar, Robert B. Yelin

The Jazz Guitar Chord Bible Complete, Warren Nunes

Jazz Guitar Chord Thesaurus, Kirk Tatnall

These are so-called "fake books," collections of lead sheets for jazz and standard tunes. They typically include the melodies in keyboard notation, chord symbols, and sometimes lyrics. I have a library of many such books collected since the 1950s when they were sold under the counter at mom-and-pop music stores. These are legally published editions and available from online bookstores.

Just Standards Real Book, Unknown

The Ultimate Jazz Fake Book, Unknown

The Real Book Sixth Edition, Unknown

From the Author

Thank you for reading *teach yourself... Rhythm Jazz Guitar*.

If you enjoyed this book—or even if you didn't—please visit the site where you purchased it and write a brief review. Your feedback is important to me and will help other readers decide whether to read the book.

If you'd like to get notifications of new releases and special offers on my books, please join my email list at http://www.alstevens.com.

Al Stevens, 2017

al@alstevens.com

About the Author

Al Stevens is a retired author of computer programming books. For fifteen years he was a senior contributing editor and columnist for Dr. Dobb's Journal, a leading magazine for computer programmers.

Al lives with his wife Judy and a menagerie of cats on Florida?s Space Coast where he writes by day and plays piano, guitar, string bass, and saxophone by night.

www.ingramcontent.com/pod-product-compliance
Lightning Source LLC
Chambersburg PA
CBHW050749100426
42744CB00012BA/1941